21st Century Mahan

21st
Century
Mahan

Sound Military Conclusions for the Modern Era

EDITED BY BENJAMIN F. ARMSTRONG

Naval Institute Press
Annapolis, Maryland

This book has been brought to publication with the generous assistance of
Marguerite and Gerry Lenfest.

Naval Institute Press
291 Wood Road
Annapolis, MD 21402

ISBN 978-0-87021-032-7 (eBook)
Library of Congress Cataloging-in-Publication Data

Armstrong, Benjamin F.
  21st century Mahan : sound military conclusions for the modern era / Benjamin F.
Armstrong.
      pages cm
  Includes bibliographical references.
  ISBN 978-1-61251-243-3 — ISBN 978-0-87021-032-7 (ebook) 1. Naval strategy.
2. Mahan, A. T. (Alfred Thayer), 1840-1914—Influence. 3. Naval art and science.
I. Mahan, A. T. (Alfred Thayer), 1840–1914. Works. Selections. II. Title. III. Title:
Twenty-first century Mahan.
  V163.A76 2013
  359.4—dc23

                                                    2013002178

The views, opinions, and concepts expressed in this book are the author's own.

CONTENTS

It is not the business of naval officers to write books.
—Admiral F. M. Ramsey
1893 Fitness Report for Captain Alfred Thayer Mahan

21st Century Mahan

Sound Military Conclusions

The world was experiencing rapid globalization, rising powers in Asia threatened to change the balance of power, and across the globe there was a steady increase in naval spending. In the United States, parts of the political class insisted on focusing on "the problems at home," and others feared that defense spending during tough times would result in cookie-cutter reductions across the services without the thought of strategic considerations. The decades at the turn of the twentieth century were a challenging time for the United States, just as it is at the start of the twenty-first.

More than a hundred years ago there was a historian and former naval officer who recognized and wrote on these subjects. He developed the strategic approaches to America's challenges that would lay the foundation of what some have termed "The American Century." Today that thinker is all but forgotten in strategic discussions of modern-day challenges. However, the work of Alfred Thayer Mahan is a relevant source of strategic thought that should be considered in studying solutions for the modern era.

In recent years it has become common for policymakers, naval leaders, and analysts to discount the strategic thinking and writing of Mahan. They tell us he wrote for a different time and a different United States of America. They point to his book *The Influence of Seapower Upon History*, and its focus on the Age of Sail, and say that he has nothing to offer the modern and high-technology military forces of today. We have been encouraged to dismiss him because of his focus on battleships, because of his interest in territorial expansion, or because his approaches are outdated.[1]

These writers and thinkers are mistaken. They focus solely on his most famous work and unthinkingly repeat the analysis taught by some academics. Few of these writers appear to have actually read the works of Alfred Thayer Mahan. As historian Geoffrey Till noted, "Mahan sometimes suffers from having written more than most people are prepared to read."[2] As the twentieth century approached, and after its turn, the preeminent American navalist penned more than a dozen books and several dozen articles. His writings cover a multitude of topics from combat leadership to global strategy. The world that his Navy faced at the end of the nineteenth century has many similarities to the one we live in at the opening of the twenty-first century. Much of his strategic thinking is applicable today, and it deserves consideration as the United States and its Navy face the challenges of the new century.

Turn of the Century

Mahan wrote in a time of change and international development. Increasing consumption at the end of the nineteenth century led to a general rise in standard of living for most Americans, as well as other Western nations, as compared to the rest of the world. Economic interests took a primary place in the interactions between nations. The development of rapid transportation and communication systems, driven by steam power and undersea telegraph cables, began to link the globe. Today's writers would say that the world was experiencing "globalization." Mahan wrote that "the vast increase in the rapidity of communication, [*sic*] has multiplied and strengthened the bonds knitting the interests of nations to one another, till the whole now forms an articulated system."[3] He recognized that the interaction between nations was increasingly economic. It was apparent to him that in the new century's international relations, "the maintenance of the status quo, for purely utilitarian reasons of an economical character, has gradually become the ideal."[4]

In the increasingly interconnected world that the rapid advance of modern technology was creating, Mahan perceived that while there were motives to maintain the status quo, there were also other motivations at play. He believed that the increased speed of communication, and a view of national greatness that was purely economic, tended to make the new global order excessively sensitive and open to instability. He wrote that "commerce thus, on the one hand deters from war, on the other hand it engenders conflict, fostering ambitions and strifes which tend towards armed collision."[5] In a statement reminiscent of another great strategist, Carl von Clausewitz, Mahan wrote that "war is simply a political movement, though violent and exceptional in its character."[6] Yet Mahan took a step beyond Clausewitz and tied the political, military, and economic all together. While he admitted that economic considerations can have a stabilizing effect on world affairs, he also pointed out that although "logically separable, in practice the political, commercial, and military needs are so intertwined that their mutual interaction constitutes one problem."[7] Economic or commercial motivations could drive a nation to military conflicts just as easily as they could encourage stability in the global commons.

Looking East

With these conclusions as background, Mahan looked at the world in an attempt to determine the next area of great conflict. His focus settled on Asia. A century before Thomas Friedman wrote that the rise of Asia demonstrated the flattening of the global political landscape, Mahan suggested that Japan, India, and China would become central players in a great economic and political conflict with the West. Mahan knew that the economic and political could not be separated from the military, and he saw trouble in the future. He wrote that, "as we cast our eyes in any direction, there is everywhere a stirring, a rousting from sleep," in the non-Western world and a craving for the two advantages of the West at the turn of the last century: "power and material prosperity."[8]

The early development of Japan, and the Japanese adoption of some parts of Western culture and economics, was his first indicator. He also saw the population and rise of India as having great potential. He saw in both countries the chance that they might adopt important portions of Western culture, resulting in what he called a "conversion."

China, however, was a different story. Mahan admitted that the Western world knew less about China in general, but he pointed out that experience had already shown a forceful and determined character in the Chinese people. He recognized that there was a general conservatism in Chinese culture, and he wrote that "comparative slowness of evolution may be predicated, but that which for so long has kept China one, amid many diversities, may be counted upon in the future to insure a substantial unity of impulse." He feared that China would lead a rejection of Western values and would pull the other future powers of Asia toward a conflict with the West.[9]

Because other parts of the world aspired toward the power and material prosperity of the West, Mahan saw the areas of conflict beginning in the realm of economic competition. He saw that access to markets, as well as to the raw materials needed for production, is at the heart of economic competition between nations. He wrote that "as the interaction of commerce and finance shows a unity in the modern civilized world, so does the struggle for new markets and for predominance in old, [sic] reveal the unsubdued diversity."[10] As the large populations of Asia struggled to gain their economic strength, and to achieve the power and prosperity of the West, Mahan saw that they were likely to do so based on their own cultural norms and not those of the West. Of China and the West he said that "they are running as yet on wholly different lines, springing from conceptions radically different."[11] In the future he believed that these differences would result in competition and conflict.

Mahan believed that the world was "at the beginning of this marked movement" toward economic competition that would bring nations into political and military conflict with one another.[12] He reminded his readers that "those who want will take, if they can, not merely from motives of high policy and as legal opportunity offers, but for the simple reasons that they have not, that they desire, and that they are able."[13] Because of this, and because of the fact that "we are not living in a perfect world, and we may not expect to deal with imperfect conditions by methods ideally perfect," Mahan turned his attention to military policy.[14]

Preparing for Conflict

As the United States approached the beginning of the twentieth century, Alfred Thayer Mahan looked at his nation's military policy and saw disaster on the horizon. If his analysis of international affairs was correct—if the United States faced a time of rapid globalization, rising powers from the non-Western world, and particularly the awakening giants of China and Asia—then the military policy of the United States was in desperate need of an overhaul.

With these conclusions as a background, Mahan was living in a United States that considered the Army more important to national security than the Navy. He lamented the fact that "of invasion, [sic] in any real sense of the word we run no risk, and if we did it must be at sea . . . yet the force of men in the navy is smaller, by more than half, than that in the army."[15] He felt that it was clear that overseas commerce, overseas political relationships, and commercial maritime routes would dominate as "the primary objects of external policy of nations." It was only logical that "the instrument for the maintenance of policy directed upon these objects is the Navy."[16] The nations of Europe, at the time the great powers of the world, were on the same page as Mahan. He noticed that the newspapers and political journals of Europe were showing an appreciation for the importance of naval forces in the new century, and it was reflected in the growth of naval spending and sizes of fleets.[17]

Approaching the question of military organization for the United States, Mahan wrote that it was wrong to start with the sizes of the armies and navies of the world with the idea of creating a mathematical equation that would allow the United States to ensure its own superiority. Instead he felt that it was better to determine "what there is in the political status of the world, including not only the material interests but the temper of nations, which involves a reasonable, even though remote, prospect of difficulties which may prove insoluble except by war." Those prospective difficulties provided the guidance for the strategic vision of the nation. He continued by saying that "it is not the most probable of danger, but the most formidable that must be selected as measuring the degree of military precautions to be embodied in the military preparations thenceforth to be maintained."[18]

Mahan believed that, because of the challenges faced by the United States at the start of the twentieth century, a military organization that favored naval power was the most strategically viable course for his country. The most reasonable "prospective difficulties" that the United States would face would be overseas. The most formidable danger, an attack on the United States itself, would have to come from overseas. He wrote that "every danger of a military character to which the United States is exposed can be met best outside her own territory—at sea. Preparedness for naval war—preparedness against naval attack and for naval offence—is preparedness for anything that is likely to occur."[19]

The Modern Mahanian World

While the technology of today's U.S. Navy has developed far beyond anything Mahan could have conceived, it is unlikely that it would surprise him. He recognized the importance of what he called "rapid mechanization," or what we call the development of high technology. The political state of the world that the United States faces today, also, would not have surprised Mahan. Globalization, rising powers, Asian development, and the impact of technology were just as important a century ago as they are today.

As the defense budgets of the United States and the European community contract in the early twenty-first century, it is important that policymakers understand the world that they face and consider the strategic questions that should guide their decisions. Alfred Thayer Mahan laid out the questions that should be asked when facing similar challenges. Answering them can help create a sound foundation for any new approach to defense spending as the twenty-first century progresses.

First, what in the "temper of nations" around the world could lead to a reasonable expectation of armed conflict? Considerations should include growing movements in the non-Western world for freedom and representative government, and the potential conflict of that temperament with the spread of radical and religious ideologies. Thought must also be given to the role played by smaller nations such as Iran and North Korea when they attempt to exploit the divisions and uncertainty introduced by the most recent round of globalization. Also, the growing potential for economic competition between the rising powers of China, India, and Brazil, and established powers like the United States and European Union, raises a reasonable expectation of conflict in the future.

Second, what is the most formidable of these potential conflicts? While the clash between authoritarian governments and the building momentum of freedom movements is likely to create conflict, it produces little direct strategic threat to the United States as a nation. Likewise, attempts to exploit international instability by regional powers will probably impact American policy and interests, but not the security of the country's borders. The prospect of an armed conflict between the United States and China, sparked by economic competition, is a very formidable challenge and a more direct threat to the United States. Mahan would not suggest ignoring the first two reasonable expectations; however, according to his strategic approach, the focus should be on the final and most formidable threat to American security.

The makers of defense policy today face similar challenges in the development of sound, strategically shaped, defense policy as Mahan lamented in his days. The tendency in the halls of power to try and avoid making hard decisions has not changed. As the United States approaches significant cuts in defense spending, there have already been calls to divide the cuts evenly between the budgets of the services, ignoring Mahan's warning against the great risks of such a policy. The rise of counterinsurgency strategy and doctrine, and a growing desire by some policymakers to apply that operational and tactical template to all defense problems, also demonstrates a potential risk of the pendulum that the captain warned about.

Reading the Forgotten Strategist

There are two particular reasons that Mahan's work has slowly fallen out of favor. First, his writing style isn't particularly modern or easy for twenty-first-century readers. This is especially true of his books and longer works of history, including his seminal work, *The Influence of Sea Power Upon History 1660–1815*. Mahan's own son admitted that reading his work frequently can be a laborious process. Mahan wrote in his autobiography *From Sail to Steam* that his attempt to clarify every assertion and qualify every statement tended to make his work thorough, but difficult, reading.

Second, for a generation of students of military history and international affairs, as well was naval officers, the teaching of Alfred Thayer Mahan's work has focused on two things that appear to lack relevance in the modern world: the importance of battleships and the main battlefleet, as well as a focus on the United States' entry into the colonial system at the start of the twentieth century, with the annexation of the Hawaiian Islands, the possession of the Philippines following the Spanish American War, and the construction of the Panama Canal.

Because many naval analysts and officers suffer from a measure of technological determinism, Mahan's alleged focus on a vessel that has long been replaced in the fleets of the world causes many to dismiss his writing as irrelevant. The lecture notes and book chapters that serve as the foundation of their understanding of Mahan generally support this interpretation. These analysts tell us that the advancement of technology has overtaken the strategist's ideas because he doesn't account for the speed of aviation or the importance of precision guided munitions. Colonial possessions, and imperial approaches to global affairs, aren't in vogue with students of international relations and policy at the start of this century any more than big-gun battleships. Because many students are taught that battleships and colonies make up the heart of Mahan's writing, he is frequently discounted as being of little consequence to discussions of today's challenges.

21st Century Mahan: Sound Military Conclusions for the Modern Era takes its title from a quote in Mahan's book *Armaments and Arbitration,* published in 1911. He wrote that "the study of military history lies at the foundation of all sound military conclusions and practices."[20] Looking in retrospect at the history that Mahan wrote, and the strategic legacy he left through his works, will help illuminate the global challenges we face at the start of this century, just as his work did originally at the start of the last century.

The purpose of this book is to help return the discussion of Alfred Thayer Mahan as a strategist and naval thinker to our time, and to point out the importance of his writings and principles when approaching modern-day challenges. The five essays from Mahan that make up the bulk of this book have been selected in order to address the two major reasons that his writing has fallen out of favor: readability and relevance.

Many of the articles that he wrote for magazines, such as *Harpers* and Britain's *National Review,* are more concise and approachable than the long historical treatments of conflicts like the War of 1812 and the American Revolution that he published in book form. The language in the essays is clearer because he knowingly approached a readership that was non-specialist, and he didn't feel the same need to smother his audience in details and caveats as he sometimes did in his longer books. The length of the essays allows readers to digest his writing in smaller amounts and gives time for greater reflection.

Each of the five essays selected for *21st Century Mahan* covers a subject that is central to the debates and discussions of national, military, and naval policy in the twenty-first century. They illustrate the connections between globalization and the fleet, lessons on naval administration, military leadership, teaching officers and sailors, and they challenge the conventional wisdom about Mahan's ideas.

The world of Mahan is today. The international challenges that sparked Mahan's writing and thinking in the previous century are strikingly similar to those that we face now. The basic principles of national strategy and armed conflict have not changed, despite the rapid advancement of technology and a new version of globalization that has left the colonial model behind. Capt. Alfred Thayer Mahan wrote about much more than simply battleships and overseas colonies. His work provides illumination and insight that would serve today's military leadership as well as the commonly discussed lessons of other great strategic thinkers such as Von Clausewitz or Sun Tzu. To help face a world of globalization, rising powers, increasing worldwide spending on naval forces, and a rapidly developing Asia, students, officers, and policymakers will all benefit from reading the works of America's great strategic thinker, Alfred Thayer Mahan.

CHAPTER ONE

Management, Administration, and Naval Leadership

Today's military leaders are just as likely to be students of business theory and management practice as of history or international affairs. Since the end of the Cold War there has been a movement in some circles claiming that the networked battlefield of the new century can be best approached through these disciplines. Some of the first links between the fields of business and war were made by Adm. Arthur Cebrowski in his study of network-centric warfare.[1] Alfred Thayer Mahan disagreed. In Mahan's view, there was a place for what we call today business or organizational theory—what Mahan referred to as administration—but it should never be the driving force behind naval or military decisions, and it always had to be kept in check.

In 1903 Mahan tackled the subject of the role of administration directly. In May of that year he wrote an essay entitled "The Principles of Naval Administration: Historically Considered," which in turn was published in the *National Review* in June. Mahan's goal was to write for the general audience that would be reading the magazine, but in doing so he realized that he had simplified his thinking and made it clearer to naval professionals, as well. The article was republished as the lead essay in his collection *Naval Administration and Warfare: Some General Principles*, in 1908.

"The Principles of Naval Administration" begins with a discussion of the essentially civil role of administration, even though in the Department of the Navy the positions are generally held by military officers. Mahan tells his readers that there is a natural conflict between the military officer and the administrator, and that can be a strength of the system. He also writes:

> The military man having to do the fighting, considers that the chief necessity; the administrator equally naturally tends to think the smooth running of the machine the most admirable quality. Both are necessary; but the latter cannot obtain under the high pressure of war unless in peace the contingency of war has dictated its system. There is a quaint, well-worn story, which yet may be new to some readers, of an administrator who complained that his office was working admirably until war came and threw everything out of gear.[2]

Mahan believed that, when given the opportunity, the smooth operation of the essentially bureaucratic tasks of administration would overwhelm military considerations and the necessities of warfare. For that reason military officers, especially those on staff duty, would need to constantly guard against the idea that the "economical working of the office" was more important than the impact on the ability of combat forces to do their job. Mahan believed that it wouldn't take long for officers in staff positions to be corrupted by the civil administrative system. Time served on staff duty, away from combat units, "tends to deaden the intimate appreciation of naval exigencies." As a result, officers needed to ask themselves constantly if they were helping deployed naval forces to be ready for combat, or if they were helping the administrative system to run more smoothly and acceptably to civilians and politicians. He reminded officers that "the habit of the arm-chair easily prevails over that of the quarter-deck; it is more comfortable."[3]

From his discussion of the challenges of keeping a proper balance between military considerations and administrative ease—a balance that places the greatest importance on the military—Mahan moves on to discussing the overall organization of navies. The essay tells us first how the Royal Navy had been organized and governed administratively from its founding through the start of the twentieth century. Mahan then compares the British system to the system that had developed in the United States.

The discussion of the two systems covers a number of valuable areas. Mahan supported the American system that always placed final control of the Navy in the hands of one civilian. He compared it to a British system that was run by committee at times, at other times by a single officer, and at others by a single civilian. Mahan believed that having one person in charge encouraged responsibility and accountability, while ensuring that person was a civilian maintained the proper relationship between elected officials and military officers in the American system.

Mahan also discusses the bureau system, which had been adopted by the United States to run the Navy. While he appreciated the expert advice that bureau chiefs could give the secretary of the Navy, Mahan recognized that the chiefs were also in competition with one another constantly for funding. Although the competition could, at times, drive positive results, it also ensured that the secretary didn't always receive the best advice as the chiefs attempted to outmaneuver one another.

Mahan's detailed examination of the rise of the British and American systems of naval administration has important relevance in the twenty-first century. As the size of the fleet has continued to shrink since the end of the Cold War, the number of flag officers and their large, associated staffs appears only to have grown. Mahan's discussion shows us ways to encourage responsibility and accountability, while also looking for the most efficient system. His article can shed light across the entire Department of Defense, as shrinking budgets will dictate a reassessment of the organization of the military across the board.

During wartime, Mahan points out that the relationship between military considerations and administration is easy, because commanders on the field of battle always have the immediacy of combat to help them focus their staff on proper priorities. In peacetime, however, it is a different story. As the wars of the first decade of the twenty-first century are brought to a close, and budgetary pressure increases on the military, today's uniformed officers should heed Mahan's warning that, outside of war, "administration then becomes the bigger and more imposing activity, with an increasing tendency to exist for itself rather than for the military purposes which are its sole reason for existence."[4]

THE PRINCIPLES OF NAVAL ADMINISTRATION

February 1903

Definition is proverbially difficult, but the effort to frame it tends to elicit fullness and precision of comprehension. What then do we mean by administration in general, and what are the several and diverse conceptions that enter into the particular idea of naval administration?

Considered generally, administration is, I suppose, an office committed to an individual, or to a corporate body, by some competent authority, to the end that it may supply a particular want felt. At a point in its historical development a country finds that it needs a navy. To supply the need it institutes an office. For the special purpose it vests so much of its own power as may be necessary in a particular person or persons, and requires that he, or they, supply to it a navy. The original grant of powers carries the reasonable implication that they will be maintained and amplified as occasion requires. That is the duty of the State to the administration it has created; and for that reason the State—which in Great Britain and the United States is ultimately the people—requires to understand what is involved in the office, for the existence and working of which it has made itself responsible. It is not, indeed, requisite to follow out all the minutiae of action, but it is essential to comprehend the several great principles which should receive recognition in the completed scheme; which of them should govern, and which should be subordinate in function. If these relations be properly adjusted, the system is sound and may be trusted to work itself, provided continuous care be taken in the choice of persons. The engine will be good; but the engineers must be good also.

Naval administration has another side, and one more commonly familiar. It faces two ways, towards the nation and towards the service. It ministers to the country a navy; but in so doing it embraces numerous functions, and engages in numerous activities, the object of which is the navy itself, in the supply of all that is needed for its healthy existence. It is to these in their entirety that the term naval administration is most commonly applied. Thus viewed the subject is complex and demands a certain amount of analysis; in order that by the recognition of the leading needs and principles involved there may be a clearer understanding of their individual bearings and relative importance. It will be found here, as in most practical callings, that efficiency depends upon a full appreciation of elements which, though essential, are conflicting in tendency, and upon due weight being given to each.

Administration being a term of very general application, it will be expected that that of the navy should present close analogies, and even points of identity, with other forms of administration; for instance, that in it, as elsewhere, efficiency of result will be better secured by individual responsibility than by collective responsibility. But, along with general resemblance, naval administration is very clearly and sharply differentiated by the presence of an element which is foreign to almost all other activities of life in countries like Great Britain and the United States. The military factor is to it not merely incidental, but fundamental; whatever other result may be achieved, naval administration has failed unless it provides to the nation an efficient fighting body, directed by well-trained men, animated by a strong military spirit. On the other hand, many of the operations connected with it differ from those common to civil life only in a certain particularity of method. This is true in principal measure of the financial management, of the medical establishment, and to a considerable though much smaller degree of the manufacturing processes connected with the production of naval material. The business routine of even the most military department of a naval administration is in itself more akin to civil than to military life: but it by no means follows that those departments would be better administered under men of civil habits of thought than by those of military training. The method exists for the result, and an efficient fighting body is not to be attained by weakening the appreciation of military necessities at the very fountain head of their supply in the administration. This necessary appreciation can be the result only of personal experience of good and bad through the formative period of life.

We find, therefore, at the very outset of our inquiry two fundamental yet opposing elements, neither of which can be eliminated. Nor can they be reconciled, in the sense of becoming sympathetic. In its proper manifestation the jealousy between the civil and military spirits is a healthy symptom. They can be made to work together harmoniously and efficiently; to complement, not to antagonize each other; provided means are taken to ensure to each its due relative precedence and weight in the determination of practical questions.

Historically, the institution and development of naval administration has been essentially a civil process, the object of which has been to provide and keep in readiness a national weapon for war. The end is war—fighting; the instrument is the navy; the means are the various activities which we group under the head of administration. Of these three, the end necessarily conditions the others. The proverb is familiar, "He who wills the end wills the means." Whatever is essential to the spirit and organization of the Navy afloat, to its efficiency for war, must find itself adequately represented in the administration, in order that the exigencies of fighting may be kept well to the front in governmental and national consideration. Since armies and navies have existed as permanent national institutions, there has been a constant struggle on the part of the military element to keep the end—fighting, or readiness to fight—superior to mere administrative considerations. This is but natural, for all men tend to magnify their office. The military man having to do the fighting, considers that the chief necessity; the administrator equally naturally tends to think the smooth running of the machine the most admirable quality. Both are necessary; but the latter cannot obtain under the high pressure of war unless in peace the contingency of war has dictated its system. There is a quaint, well-worn story, which yet may be new to some readers, of an administrator who complained that his office was working admirably until war came and threw everything out of gear.

The opposition between civil and military, necessitating their due adjustment may be said to be original, of the nature of things. It is born with naval administration. Corresponding roughly to these primary factors are the two principal activities in which administration is exerted—organization and execution. These also bear to each other the relation of means to end. Organization is not for itself, but is a means to an ultimate executive action; in the case of a navy, to war or to the prevention of war. It is, therefore, in its end—war—that organization must find the conditions dictating its character. Whatever the system adopted, it must aim above all at perfect efficiency in military action; and the nearer it approaches to this ideal the better it is. It would seem that this is too obvious for mention. It may be for mention; but not for reiteration. The long record of naval history on the side of administration shows a constant predominance of other considerations, and the abiding necessity for insisting, in season and out of season, that the one test of naval administration is not the satisfactory or economical working of the office, as such, but the readiness of the navy in all points for war. The one does not exclude the other; but there is between them the relation of greater and less.

Both organization and execution are properties alike of the active navy, the instrument for war, and of the naval administration, the means which has been constituted to create and maintain the instrument; but from their respective spheres, and in proportion to their relative nearness to the great final end of war, the one or the other characteristic is found predominant. The naval officer on board his ship, face to face with the difficulties of the profession, and in daily contact with the grim implements which remind him of the eventualities of his calling, naturally sees in organization mainly a means to an end. Some indeed fall short. The martinet is a man to whom the organization is more than a means; but he is the exception. Naval administration, on the other hand, in the common acceptation of the term, is mostly office work. It comes into contact with the Navy proper chiefly through official correspondence, less by personal intercourse with the officers concerned; still less by immediate contact with the daily life of the profession, which it learns at second hand. It consequently tends to overvalue the orderly routine and observance of the system by which it receives information, transmits orders, checks expenditure, files returns, and, in general, keeps with the service the touch of paper; in short, the organization which has been created for facilitating its own labours. In due measure these are imperatively necessary; but it is undeniable that the practical tendency is to exaggerate their importance relatively to the executive end proposed. The writer was once visiting a French captain, who in the course of the interview took up wearily a mass of papers from a desk beside him. "I wonder," said he, "whether all this is as bad with you as with us. Look at our Navy Register;" and dividing the pages into two parts, severally about one-sixth and five-sixths of the whole, he continued, "This, the smaller, is the Navy; and that is the Administration." No wonder he had papers galore; administration needs papers, as a mill needs grist.

Even in the case of naval officers entering administrative offices, the influence of prolonged tenure is in the same direction. The habits of a previous lifetime doubtless act as a check, in proportion to the strength they have acquired in the individual. They serve as an invaluable leaven. not only to his own thought but to that of his associates. Nevertheless, the experience is general that permanence in an office essentially civil tends to deaden the intimate appreciation of naval exigencies; yet upon this alone can thrive that sympathy between the administrative and executive functions of the navy which is requisite to efficiency. The habit of the arm-chair easily prevails over that of the quarter-deck; it is more comfortable. For this reason, in the best considered systems, a frequent exchange between the civil and military parts of their profession, between the administrative offices and the army or fleet, is thought expedient for officers who show aptitude for the former. It is better for them personally, better for the administration, and consequently better for the service at large. It prevails extensively in the United States Navy, where it is frequently the subject of ill-instructed outside criticism on the score of sea officers being on "shore duty." Without asserting that the exact proportions of service are always accurately observed, it may be confidently affirmed that the interchange between the civil and military occupations tends to facilitate the smooth working of both, by promoting mutual understanding of conditions and difficulties.

The subject of this paper is not the navy, although that as a military organization has necessarily its own interior administration. What we have here to consider is an organization essentially civil, although it has naval men as individual members and a military body as the subject of its activities. In the United States the naval administration has thus been continuously regarded as a civil occupation, under the two principal forms given it since the adoption of the Constitution. In its origin, in 1798, the Secretary of the Navy was the sole functionary and a member of the President's Cabinet. The Board of Naval Commissioners, which from 1815 to 1842 was charged with all the ministerial duties under the Secretary, was composed of three naval captains; but when one of them, Captain Charles Morris, was selected for a temporary command at sea, he insisted upon resigning his office of Commissioner, because "I believed that the exercise of the military duties of a captain, whilst holding a district commission of a civil character, would be exceedingly disagreeable to the feelings of the officers, even if legal." When the Board of Naval Commissioners gave way to the Bureau System which now exists, the same civil character inhered, and incumbents of Bureaus were at times taken directly from civil life. In the British Navy the understanding was the same concerning the civil nature of duties assumed by naval officers under the organization which we call Naval Administration. One of the earliest notable incidents of Nelson's life, when a young captain, was a flat refusal to obey the order of an officer much his senior, when holding the local position of a Dockyard Commissioner in the civil administration of the Navy. The administration of the British Navy in this and cognate matters was then in fact distinctly styled "civil." It had a large history, characterized through great part of its course by incessant struggle with the military administration, either incorporate in the single person of the Lord High Admiral, or more usually placed in commission as the Board of Admiralty. The latter was nominally superior, but commonly strove in vain to assert its authority against an interest strongly entrenched in a traditional position.

In the United States there never has been such formal duality of functions as was produced by the gradual evolution of the British system, which, like the British Constitution, rather grew than was framed. The effect in the latter, by the existence of the two Boards, was to illustrate and intensify an antagonism always sufficiently rooted in the opposition between civil and military. Thence resulted practical evils which finally compelled the formal abolition of the Civil Board, and the transfer of its duties to the Board of Admiralty, suitably reinforced for that purpose by a number of subordinate technical experts, not members of the Board, and no longer so associated together as to hold the power of concerted action which attaches to an organic group. There was thus restored, or it should rather be said established, the unity essential to all military administration; the unity in this case of a single, regularly constituted Board. From this, however, the logic of facts has gradually evolved the accepted principle of a supreme individual responsibility, that of the First Lord, who is a member of the Government. He is responsible for all the business of the Admiralty; while each of the other members has his separate functions, for the discharge of which he is responsible to the First Lord, although, as we are informed by a recent high authority, "this responsibility is not easy to define."

In Great Britain, therefore, as in the United States, one man is now ultimately responsible; the Secretary of the Navy in the one State, the First Lord in the other. The difference between the two systems is that the United States Secretary, belonging to no Board, has to deal with subordinates only, not with associates. The First Lord, as member of the Board, which assembles frequently, necessarily meets his assistants not merely singly, but together; thus undergoing an influence much weightier and more complex than that of consulting at convenience single men, each of whom appears before him strong only in his natural strength of character, modified by the military habit of submission. We are told of Sir Robert Walpole that he avoided as much as possible calling Cabinet councils, lest they should furnish the elements of an opposition. The First Lord doubtless may absent himself from the meetings of the Board, if he will, but the spirit of the system would in that case be violated. Like the American Secretary of the Navy, he is, by custom now almost invariable, a civilian. Regarding the expert professional members of the naval administration as subordinate, as they properly are in both systems, it is evident that the British tends to a greater influence of the military element. It is, however, influence, not authority; two powers of very different natures. There appears to be in practice considerable indeterminateness as to the executive functions of the Admiralty Board as a body, an absence of definition characteristically English; but the single ultimate responsibility of the First Lord necessarily carries with it single uncontrolled authority. Without that it is idle to speak of responsibility.

In main outline, both systems consist of a single responsible civil head with a number of professional subordinates, among whom are apportioned the several executive duties of the naval administration. The British provides in addition, by distinct implication and by usual practice, a consultative body, which does not exist in the American. Although it is, of course, open to any American Secretary to call such into being for his own assistance, its opinions would not give him, being its creator, the moral support, nor exert over him the influence, that inheres in one established by statute. This difference tends to emphasize the single responsibility of the United States Secretary of the Navy, and probably has the result of producing in him a greater sense of accountability. He has no associates; the British First Lord has. It is interesting to note that each method reproduces the specific political genius of the nation. In the United States the executive power of the general government rests explicitly in one man; so also that of the Navy Department. In Great Britain the executive government rests in a Committee of Parliament, of whom one is Prime Minister; the administration of the navy is also technically "in commission," whatever may be the practical outcome as to responsibility.

There is yet another result of the Board system as compared with ours, in that an officer of experience writing about it can say, "There is no real separation of the duties of the Lords of the Admiralty; they are not heads of departments rigidly denned; the operations they superintend are closely inter-related." "The happy constitution of the Board enables it to handle a mass of business now grown to vast complexity, without splitting it up into over-specialized departments, presided over by independent chiefs with duties and offices sharply and precisely defined." The contrast here is pronounced; for while the duties of the bureau-chiefs, who are the professional subordinates of the American civil head of department, are necessarily closely inter-related, because concerning the same common profession, they are nevertheless sharply defined, and their chiefs mutually independent. This condition emphasizes their individual responsibility; but it also fosters a separateness of interest and of action which by some officers in the United States Navy has been considered to be a fruitful cause of bad administration. The unifying force is not the consultation and interaction of a Board, but the authority of a single head; and he, being frequently inexpert in naval practical life, is not always best fitted to comprehend the relative value of technical or military points, or to adjust to the best advantage of the service the conflicting demands which the bureau-chiefs represent.

We are here in presence of a great difficulty of naval administration; which is, to attain and preserve substantial unity of executive action, while at the same time providing for the distribution among several individuals of a mass of detailed duties, beyond the power of one man to discharge. This need of unity applies not only to high considerations of policy, or a few larger questions of administration. It enters into every dockyard, and above all into every component unit of the fleet. In the United States seven bureaus have a part and a claim in every ship that is planned. When it is remembered that the necessarily contracted capacity of a ship of war has made the disposition of space in every period a difficult problem, it will be understood that in our day, of complicated construction and armament, we have in the various bureau demands the elements of a conflict that may aptly be called intestine. To this must be added, qualifying and, to some extent, contesting the whole result, the military requirements of the navy outside of the administration, which has the combatant duties pressing upon its attention. Nautical qualities, armament and armour, speed, coal capacity, provisions and stores, accommodation of crew, sanitary provision, all these, with many details attendant on each, have their special representative in the central general administration. Beyond these, but not specifically represented there, is the military body, which demands, or should demand, observance of the pre-eminent consideration that the ship should be in all respects fitted for the special function she is to fulfill in a fleet; that cruisers, for instance, should not only be fast, but in all things contrived for celerity in their actions; that battleships, being meant to act together, should not only be individually good, but essentially homogeneous, especially in tactical qualities. In the report of one of the early American Secretaries it was noted, as being to the grave discredit of the Civil Administration of the British Navy, that the existence of "numerous distinct classes of the same rate, as well in their hulls as in masts, sails, and equipment, *and in a still greater degree in their qualities for combined action,* demonstrates the prevalence of caprice and prejudice, instead of science and system." Even the interchange of parts and of stores, between vessels of the same class, upon which he further comments, though perhaps less important to-day, is a consideration not out of date.

Over all hovers, not unhealthfully, the consideration of expense. A very high official in a navy which entrusts to a naval officer the final decisions as to the assemblage of qualities said once to me: "With practically unlimited money, such as your lucky nation can give, one may go to extremes in experiments; but limited as we are in means, and with large establishments, it is necessary to digest ideas, to compromise on size, and to settle on a type." In the support thus given to unity of design, in ensuring a just predominance to military considerations, considerations that think first of the day of battle, of the months of campaign, of the services of the scout, of the evolutions of the fleet, of the need for numbers as well as for individual size, it can be seen that the pressure of economy may be an invaluable ally.

The two great oppositions inherent in naval administration—civil *versus* military, unity of action against multiplicity of activities—are but a reflection of the essential problem of warfare. A saying has been attributed by Thiers to the great Napoleon, that the difficulty of the Art of War consists in concentrating in order to fight, and disseminating in order to subsist. There is no other, he said, aphoristically. The problem is one of embracing opposites. That we have here on the one hand unity of action, and on the other diffusion of activities, in the harmonious combination of which the problem of war consists, is probably plain enough; but it may be less obvious how the civil element enters where all is apparently military. Nevertheless it is there in full administrative force. The army concentrated to fight is the army unified in the final action for which it exists; the military element in full vigour and predominance, the question of subsistence reduced for the moment to the barest minimum, yet not even so wholly discarded. The army disseminated to subsist is a force for which unity of action is temporarily subordinated to the exigency that so many men cannot live on the resources of a narrow district, in which it camps or through which it marches, nor conveniently receive even its own daily supplies from a single centre. Given over now chiefly to subsisting, against the next call for action, the administrative bodies, civil in function if military in rank, assume the predominant role. Nevertheless, even here military necessity exercises the prior control; for the position of the several corps, if stationary, or the lines of march of the several columns, if in movement, must be so disposed that concentration may be effected with a rapidity which shall defy an enemy's attempt to strike any division in detail. This military requirement, though latent, subjects to itself the whole administrative regulation, whatever the inconvenience.

In operations of actual war the predominance of the military end in view is easily maintained, and is personified in the officer in chief command. The principle is settled that in the field all purely administrative bodies, commonly called staff corps, are under his orders. It is less easy in peace to ensure the due balance between the end and the means; between the action, and the activities which underlie action. Administration then becomes the bigger and more imposing activity, with an increasing tendency to exist for itself rather than for the military purposes which are its sole reason for existence. One of the greatest military administrators afloat that the British Navy has ever known was Admiral the Earl of St. Vincent. Yet, when peace supervened during his tenure of office as First Lord, preoccupation with economies of administration so prevailed with him that, when war broke out again, the material of the Navy in ships and stores was so deteriorated and exhausted as to impair dangerously the efficiency of the fleets. It is not that the head has ceased to be military, for in war as in peace the military as well as the administrative head of the navy may be a civil official, as he now is in Great Britain and the United States; but warlike action having ended, the importance of keeping military necessities predominant is gradually subjected to other considerations. Yet in that predominance, in whatever way assured, is to be found the unifying principle of a military administration. In the due relation and subordination of the two ideas, military and civil, unity of action with distribution of activities too copious for one man's discharge, consists the problem of military and of naval administration. It involves execution, concerning which it is a commonplace to say that in its greatest efficiency it is the function of one solely responsible; and it involves also organization, which by its very name implies multiplicity, for organization is an assemblage of organs among which functions are apportioned.

As usual, history sheds an illuminative ray on this subject by its narrative of progress. Where a naval administrative system is the result of a natural evolution, it will usually be found to begin on a small scale, in the hands of a single person. It has then but one organ, however many the functions. As it progresses in scope and number of activities, its functions differentiate more and more and it is led to evolve organs. In the process the two ideas which we have noted will be found not only to exist, but to conflict perpetually. The subordinate functions embodied in the problem of maintenance, however distributed, tend ever to assert their independence of one another and of the end for which they severally and collectively exist. The complaint of this tendency is a part of naval history, and finds its natural voice in the military sea-going body, because that is the chief sufferer.

The naval administration of Great Britain, originating in a political organization of much lower type than now obtains, and so continuing for centuries, affords the best example of a purely natural evolution, controlled by circumstances, the successive steps of which can be very briefly told. Collated with that of the United States, the contrast illustrates by comparison. In the reign of John is first found a single official, called the Clerk of the Ships. He had from time to time subordinates; but as a matter of organization he stood alone, charged with all the duties connected with the maintenance of the king's ships. The navy, so far as it existed independently of a temporary assemblage of merchant vessels for a particular purpose, was then regarded less as national than as the personal property of the sovereign. This very rudimentary civil administration lasted to the days of Henry VIII, who throughout his life interested himself directly in the development of naval material; partly from political recognition of the value and scope of a navy for England, partly through personal bent. Mr. Oppenheim, the most searching investigator in this field, writes: "For almost thirty-eight years, nearly every year marked some advance in construction or administration, some plan calculated to make the navy a more effective fighting instrument." This close association would naturally make the ruler aware when the existing administrative system had become inadequate to the extension it had received. Hence, in the last year of his reign, Henry constituted a board of five officers, civil functionaries, among whom were distributed the various administrative duties. To this, with considerable interruptions under the first Stuarts and the Commonwealth, the care and development of the material of the navy was entrusted for nearly three centuries. The members were known as the Principal Officers, and later as the Navy Board, their work being done under the superintendence of the sovereign, directly or through a minister. The head of the navy as a military force was the Lord High Admiral; but in early days that officer was not necessarily expert in naval material, not necessarily a seaman at all, nor the office itself continuous. He was therefore entirely at a disadvantage in maintaining his side of any technical contention.

This condition lasted till the Restoration, when the Duke of York, afterwards James II, became Lord High Admiral. He was a seaman of good administrative ability, and with the personal prestige of royal blood. He revived the Navy Board under his own control. When deprived of his position, because a Roman Catholic, the office of Lord High Admiral was placed in commission; an Admiralty Board, military in character, succeeded to the authority which the Duke had established. From this time there were the two Boards, the Admiralty and the Navy, the military and the civil. The former was nominally superior; but the latter, which comprised substantially all that we call naval administration, being older and well established, succeeded in maintaining a position which has been characterized as of more than semi-independence. The result was a divided control, and antagonism between the two which represented respectively the civil and military functions; nor was this lessened by the fact that members of the Navy Board were not infrequently sea officers, who thus passed into a civil occupation, practically abandoning their former profession. The fault inhered in the system.

Divided control means divided responsibility; and that in turn means no responsibility, or at least one very hard to fix. The abuses that grew up, especially in the dockyards, the effect of which of course was transmitted to the navy that depended upon them, led to a loud outcry throughout the service towards the end of the eighteenth century; but horses are not swapped when crossing streams, and the exigencies of the great wars which ended in 1815 made it long impossible to attempt the revolutionary change needed. This was carried out in 1832 by the Government which came in with the Reform Bill of 1830. The spirit of the innovation was summarized in the expression, "Individual (undivided) Responsibility." The Navy Board disappeared altogether. The civil functions which in the process of centuries had accumulated in its hands, and had culminated by successive additions into a very numerous and loose aggregation of officials, were concentrated into five heads, having separate and independent responsibilities; in this resembling the Chiefs of Bureau in the United States Naval Administration. Each of the five was specifically under one of the members of the Admiralty Board, who thus represented that particular interest of the Navy in the Board regarded as a consultative body. Admiral Sir Vesey Hamilton writes: "This was a consolidation of functions and a subordination of the civil branches to the Admiralty as a whole . . . under the Board of Admiralty collectively and under the Lords individually." While the First Lord is a civilian, the majority of the other members of the Admiralty are naval officers. Authority, therefore, is in civil hands, while military influence enters strongly.

While I highly appreciate the value of this latter factor, particularly as the sea lords do not consequently give up their profession, but remain actively connected with it, it appears to my observation of human nature that the system has some of the disadvantages of a council of war, tending to make responsibility elusive. I question, in short, the entire soundness of a scheme which by its nature, if not by specific provision, inclines to place executive action in the hands of a consultative body. It seems to sap individual responsibility; not perhaps in subordinates, but, what is much worse, in the head, in the commander-in-chief of the administration, upon whom depend the great determinative lines of provision and of policy. In conception, the Admiralty is primarily a Board, secondarily individual members. For individual responsibility at the head, too much depends upon the personality of the First Lord, too little upon his position. Since these lines were first written, five years ago, it may fairly be inferred, from the language of the English Press, that very decisive changes of policy have been adopted which are attributed popularly, and even professionally, to the dominating influence of one of the "Sea" Lords. During a brief period in 1827, as two centuries before, an arrangement more formally ideal obtained. The Duke of Clarence, afterwards William IV, being appointed Lord High Admiral, the Admiralty Board lapsed as a board and became his council. The modification here made in deference to royal blood might well serve as a model for naval administration; a head with advisers feels responsibility more than a head with associates. It should go without saying that in any case the head must be good.

In the United States Naval Administration the head is one man, with no division of responsibility. His own superior, the President, may control his action, as may Congress by law; but this, as far as it goes, is simply a transfer of responsibility in its entirety. It is not a division. The Secretary of the Navy has no associates, but he has subordinates. In them he has capable advisers, so far as he chooses to use them; but he can transfer to them no responsibility, except that of doing as he tells them. The responsibility of decision is his alone. The law constitutes them subordinate executive officers, just as it constitutes a lieutenant in the navy; but it does not constitute them advisers, and there is in their position nothing which compels the Secretary to hear their advice, still less to accept it. Each is independent of the others, and there is nothing in law to compel conference between them. The Secretary may assemble them, or any number of them, as a board for consultation, in his presence or otherwise; but there is nothing in the system which obliges him to do so. Unity of action between several naval technical experts, each of whom is represented in the planning and maintenance of every naval vessel, and some in every element of naval military efficiency, depends entirely upon the co-ordinating force of the Secretary, who is a civilian, possibly with only more or less outside knowledge of the subject. The system provides no strictly professional unifying force, such as the Board of Admiralty, which has a numerical preponderance of combatant sea-officers, each of whom has in individual control one or more of the technical administrative departments, and may be supposed therefore to be fully informed of its arguments in any technical matter under discussion. The constitution of the Admiralty Board also ensures that all technical details and their effect upon naval efficiency shall be scrutinized from the point of view of the men who shall do the work of war. The American plan fixes the very strictest individual responsibility in the Secretary, and in his principal subordinates, the chiefs of bureau. His duties are universal and supreme, theirs sharply defined and mutually independent. This result appears to me superior to the British, but it has the defects of its qualities; not too much independence in responsibility, but, so far as the system goes, too little co-ordination. As I said of the responsibility of the First Lord, unity of action depends too much on the personality of the Secretary.

The naval administration of the United States has also a history; one less of evolution than of successive methods, compressed within a very few years. The evolution has been simply a progressive experience, with results formulated in ordinances. The navy of the War of Independence disappeared entirely, and with it the several systems upon which Congress had attempted to administer it. In the first organization of the new Government, no provision was made for a navy. When the truce between Portugal and Algiers in 1793 took from American shipping in the Mediterranean the incidental protection of the Portuguese navy, it was resolved to build six frigates; but as this was to be only a temporary force, not to be continued in case a peaceful arrangement with the piratical community could be made, the administrative care of the vessels was attached to the War Department. It was not until the oppression of the French Revolutionary Government upon neutral commerce culminated in the decree of January, 1798, making any neutral vessel lawful prize if it had on board a single article of English origin, that the United States determined to have a navy. On April 27, 1798, Congress authorized the President to build, or to obtain, twelve vessels of a force not exceeding twenty-two guns each; and on April 30 the office of Secretary of the Navy was established by law. The first Secretary entered on his duties the following June. Until the close of the War of 1812, the Secretary in person, like the Clerk of the Ships, was the naval administration. He no doubt had assistants and obtained assistance, technical and military, from experts of both classes; but function had not yet differentiated into organization, and he not only was responsible, but had to give personal attention to various and trivial details of most diverse character, which overburdened him by their mass, and prevented concentration of attention upon the really great matters of his office. A difficulty such as this of course reached its height under the pressure of war, and led to the first statutory expansion of the system.

The duties of the Secretary, as a later incumbent of the office wrote, arrange themselves under two distinct heads. First in importance are those connected with the more comprehensive interests of the State, the general policy of the navy involved in the increase of the fleet, its employment and distribution when created. Subordinate to these are the functions connected with the construction, equipment, and maintenance of naval force; the designing, building, arming, and manning of ships. These latter are strictly technical; but the policy is not. It therefore may be adequately grasped by a person without antecedent professional requirements, which the Secretary often must be.

In this analysis it is easy to recognize the dual functions of the British Admiralty and Navy Board before consolidation. It is correct as far as it goes, and was sufficiently comprehensive for the time, 1842, when it was written. The naval seaman then might, and very shortly before did, receive the ship from the builder a bare shell; he was expected to be able to mast her, rig her, stow her, mount her guns, bend her sails, as well as to take her to sea, handle her, and fight her. The military and technical parts of the profession were so closely entwined in the same men that to suggest a distinction between them, however real, would have seemed superfluous. Even in those days of very simple construction and armament, however, the evil effects of valuing the technical above the military was anticipated by some. "Keep them at sea," said Lord St. Vincent, "and they cannot help being seamen; but care must be taken to ensure efficiency at the guns." In 1812 neglect of this wise maxim showed its results to the British. Since 1842 the immense technical advances in all matters connected with naval construction, propulsion, and armament have tended, by their exaltation of the technical contribution to naval power, to depreciate in popular recognition the element of military efficiency. Yet, so long as navies remain they will exist for fighting; the military considerations being the end, they must necessarily continue supreme. Naval administration, to be successful, must in its constitution reflect this condition. A necessary antecedent to doing so is the intellectual appreciation of the relation of civil to military in a service essentially military; and not merely in the internal politics of a nation. Upon this must follow formal provision for the due representation of both in the system. This is doubly requisite, because administration, being essentially civil in function, will not of itself evolve military energy. This must be injected by design.

The American naval captains of 1815 had shown themselves thorough masters in practice of all sides of their profession, technical and military. They had learned in experience the essential underlying principles affecting the nautical qualities of ships, as distinguished from the mechanical processes of putting them together by the ship builder. They, therefore, were fitted to oversee the part of administration "connected with the construction of naval force," as well as the "equipment and maintenance." To entrust this duty to one of them, or to a board of several, was a recourse so natural that in 1801 it had been recommended by the first Secretary, after two years incumbency. "The business of the Navy Department embraces too many objects for the superintendence of one person. The public interest has suffered. The establishment of a board of three or five experienced navy officers to superintend such parts of the duties as nautical men are best qualified to understand would be a saving to the public." Such a board, by the authority that attaches to a constituted organ as distinct from the purely personal, unorganized, and unauthorized efforts of single officers, might have saved the country from the gigantic administrative mistake, essentially military in its effects on efficiency, of building gunboats to the exclusion of seagoing ships; locking up in a body of two hundred vessels, impotent, singly and collectively, officers and men sufficient, by a later Secretary's report, to man thirteen ships-of-the-line.

The recommendation of 1801 fell fruitless. There followed eight years of a President who held navies in abhorrence, as at the best barely tolerable evils. The War of 1812, with the vastly increased burden laid upon the Secretary, emphasized the necessity of relief. By an Act of February 7, 1815, there was constituted a Board of Navy Commissioners, placed explicitly under the superintendence of the Secretary; to act as his agent, or, to use the terms of the Act, "to discharge all the ministerial duties" of his office, to which further it was expressly "attached." Subordination could scarcely be more distinctly affirmed. Its composition was purely military, three sea-officers of the rank of captain, then the highest in the Navy; but its duties were civil in character, and to define them the Act quoted verbatim the terms of the law of 1798, which created the Secretary's own position: "All matters connected with the naval establishment of the United States." The "establishment" is the entire organization of the navy, dockyards and ships, material and *personnel,* from inception to completion, considered apart from its active use for national policy. The use of this completed instrument is a military attribute, and is, of course, in the hands of the constitutional Commander-in-Chief, the President, who may exercise his office through the Secretary or such other person as he selects.

There was much good in this plan. It preserved the single accountability of the Secretary, provided him with the responsible assistance of a competent board of experts, and secured due influence to military considerations in a quarter where they tend to disappear. The grave defect was that the Board's responsibility was collective, not individual; and its action in all matters was joint, not several. There was no division of executive functions. Everything done was the act of all. It needs but little experience of life to know that under such circumstances decision is inevitably slow, that action shares the defect, and that the more positive and the firmer the individual members in their convictions, the more dilatory the machine, by the protraction of discussion. Ordinarily, in practice, some corrective is found in the disposition of one or more of any three to submit to the stronger character of another; and one or two will take the most of the work for the sake of exercising all the power. But such a result neither removes the evil of a joint responsibility, nor attains the beneficial result of dividing the administrative labor. Responsibility, which should be single, was divided among three; and activities beyond the ability of one, instead of being apportioned, remained the charge of all, and therefore of each.

Thus examined, the legislation of 1815 is seen to signalize the second step in the process of evolution, which it would seem must characterize the process of a military administration that springs from and follows the natural development of national wants. First the one man, the agent of the government; the seed in which, for the time, are embraced all the potential administrative functions. These in last analysis are reduced to two—the civil and military; all purely technical work falling under the former head. As the office grows, and outstrips the knowledge and power of one man, the next step is to provide him a body of assistants to take upon them severally and collectively the distinctively technical work, which the actual incumbent, either through ignorance or pressure of occupation, is unable to discharge. The Principal Officers of Henry VIII represent the same stage as the Navy Commissioners of the United States.

This first differentiation brings out at once the fact that, whatever the personal status of the chief, whether civil or military, his office is essentially military; for in the distribution of functions there is necessarily reserved to his immediate care just those which are essentially military: the direction of the navy, when created. All that relates to the establishment, to the creation and maintenance of the fleet and dockyards, is the particular charge of the technical assistants; and this is essentially a civil function, even though the officers entrusted with it be military men. This is the essence of the step taken by Henry VIII, when he called into being the Principal Officers, who became the Navy Board. In the then comparatively simple organization of the state, the sovereign, who was the actual principal and head of the office, instituted in the place of a single inexpert official a body of technical expert agents, answerable to himself in person, or to his representative. In the military direction they had no share; it remained in his hands, to be exercised directly or by such person as he might designate. Quite unconsciously, in both the British and American navies, by the simple logic of facts and felt necessities, and not as a result of previous analysis, the first expansion comes by aiding the head of the navy in the technical cares of the establishment, and leaving to him in their entirety the military attributes of the service. Although the American Secretary is by personal status a civilian, and retains full supervisory control of all technical matters, his immediate duties are comprehensively military. They have so remained since the first expansion of his administrative staff.

The tree of naval administration in the United States had thus begun to grow. It had put forth a stem in which were latent the branches that were yet to be. The merits and defects of the scheme have been indicated. The lapse of time emphasized shortcomings, and gave rise to complaints which increased yearly in volume. The Secretary, however, could maintain a judicial attitude towards the whole controversy, because it involved simply the best means of giving him the technical assistance needed. His official supremacy had been preserved, and was not threatened. In the discussion preceding the Act of 1815, the suggestion that he should be, *ex-officio*, the president of his board of technical experts, had been advanced by Commodore Decatur, whose distinguished name was supported in this by the equally strong ones of Perry, Warrington, and David Porter. The proposition was renewed in Congress in 1820, but the committee to whom it was referred placed the matter succinctly on the proper basis. "If the Secretary were a constituted part of the Board," a member among other members, "and at the same time possessed the control and superintendence of its proceedings, the commissioners would be little more than advisory, and in that proportion bereft of responsibility." If, on the contrary, he was simply a presiding officer, with a casting vote, "the benefit derived from the superintendence of one officer over others, under distinct responsibilities, would be entirely lost."

The corporate direct responsibility of the Board, under and to the Secretary, had been thus by statute preserved distinct and unimpaired. Later secretaries were therefore able to discuss the question of modification without sense of personal jealousy, as distinguished from official interest; and the change which constituted the next stage of development was recommended on the ground of well-proved faults in the system, not in individuals. "Not only has there been defect of individual responsibility to the public, but a vast accumulation of labor; since each member, being answerable alike for the action of the whole, became equally involved in an obligation to take personal cognizance of everything that was done. Under these circumstances it has been impossible to go through the great and increasing mass of business which inevitably devolved upon them with the decision and promptitude required." As the nation grew the naval administration had expanded; and inherent errors of system, tolerable on a small scale, became unendurable on a large.

Mr. Paulding, the Secretary, whose words written in 1839 have just been quoted, recommended the adoption of measures to ensure individual responsibility, which, it will be recalled, was the watchword of the corresponding change of system in the British administration in 1832. He emphasized also the need of a division of labor, "a classification and distribution of duties," which likewise was a distinct, though not the dominant, note of the British reformation. In this third stage of evolution there continues in the two nations the parallelism of cause and effect noted in the second. The action of each, however, was modified by its constitutional tradition, and the American was more radical than the British. The board system disappeared altogether, giving place to that of bureaus, mutually independent. No statutory provision for their co-operation exists, except in the supreme control of the Secretary. The essence of the new system was the constitution, under a single head, of several distinct agents, with duties sharply defined, and with individual responsibility. Among these was to be divided a mass of work, hitherto in charge of a single body, which both in executive action and in responsibility had been collective, not individual.

The details of this system, which still obtains, are relatively unimportant; but a brief statement of their historical development throws light upon the general problem of naval administration. Mr. Paulding recommended three bureaus, corresponding in number to the former commissioners. To one he assigned the construction, equipment, and maintenance of ships of war; to the second the maintenance and development of navy yards, hospitals, magazines, etc.; to the third the purchase, manufacture, and supply of stores of all kinds to the navy. These will be seen to correspond to (1) the naval establishment afloat, (2) to that ashore, and (3) to the furnishing of supplies for both. Over each of the first two he placed a sea-officer, with one technical subordinate; this assistant to the first to be a naval constructor, to the second a civil engineer. For the third bureau there was to be a "chief,"—a term evidently chosen to admit a civilian,—and under him three technical subordinates, viz.: a naval captain as inspector of ordnance, a naval captain as hydrographer, and a surgeon to superintend the provision of medical stores. This differentiation of the duties of the Board into three branches represents a minimum of change; while the association of technical subordinates to each of the three heads so much resembles the British Admiralty scheme of 1832 as to suggest irresistibly that the Secretary had had this under consideration; as he very properly might. His successor, however, thought that the duties thus distributed would be too much for the several bureaus; and of course individual responsibility, though expressed by statute, ceases to be actual when the load imposed is more than one man can bear.

This raises again the question, irrepressible because one of proportion, between unity of action and a distribution of activities, framed to ensure individual responsibility. The more numerous the bureaus, the more numerous the discordant wills and interests that must be made to act together; but if they be too few, and their several charges too weighty, there results for the chiefs, as for the Secretary before 1815, the necessity of devolving work on non-responsible subordinates. Responsibility lapses. The present (1903) Congress has had to review the same line of thought, with reference to the proposition of a recent Secretary to consolidate three of the bureaus now existing. Consolidation would tend to bring their several activities into harmony; but on the other hand there is the question whether the whole might not be too much for one man's reasonable responsibility. It is to be remembered that the responsibility of a bureau chief is more precise, more detailed and immediate, than the general responsibility of the Secretary, just because the field allotted to him is restricted. There is the further question, more urgent in public than in private business, as to the amount of power involving expenditure to be left in a single hand. After discussion, Congress in 1842 established five bureaus, and in 1862, under the pressure of the War of Secession, increased them to eight, the number which now exists. The history of the considerations which governed this further development, though instructive and useful, is not essential. When first instituted, it was stated specifically that the bureaus were not intended to perform any more or different duties than those heretofore entrusted to the Board of Commissioners. As the functions of the latter had been defined, in 1815, in words taken from the Act of 1798, constituting the office of Secretary of the Navy, continuity of legislation was preserved throughout; above all in the important matter of not impairing the sole control of the Secretary. The aim was simply to facilitate business by a division of labor, ensuring at the same time personal responsibility everywhere.

It is to the spirit, and the underlying principles, that I have thought it instructive to direct attention, rather than to the details of their application, in the subdivision of administrative work. It has been wisely observed by Sir John Seeley that "public understanding is necessarily guided by a few large, plain, simple ideas. When great interests are plain, and great maxims of government unmistakable, public opinion may be able to judge securely even in questions of vast magnitude." The United States system of naval administration has progressed successively, and without breach of legislative continuity, from the simple rudimentary organ, the one man, in whom all functions as well as all responsibility were centered, through the phase of a complex organ with aggregate functions and responsibilities, defined, but still undifferentiated, into an organization elaborate in form, if not final in development. The process has been from first to last consistent in principle. The sole control and single responsibility of the Secretary—the representative of the President—have been preserved throughout, and all other responsibility is, and has been, not only subordinate to him but derivative from him, as a branch derives its being from the root. Moreover, consistency has also been maintained in restricting the administration thus evolved to the civil function which it essentially is. From the first departure, in the institution of the Board of Commissioners, to the present time, it has not had military authority properly so called. It has had necessary authority in matters pertaining to a military establishment, but it has had no direction of activities in themselves essentially military; that has remained with the Secretary, and is by him transferred only to officers properly military in function. Finally, the principle of particular responsibility has been strictly followed. Within the limits of the duty assigned, the corporate responsibility of the Board in its day was, and the individual responsibility of each bureau chief now is, as certain and defined as that of the Secretary.

The defect of the system is that no means is provided for co-ordinating the action of the bureaus, except the single authority of the Secretary. This, in his beginning days of inexperience, together with his preoccupations with the numerous collateral engagements attendant upon all positions of public responsibility, will most usually be inadequate to the task. To indicate a defect is not to prescribe a remedy; and the purpose of this article is to show things as they are, not to advocate particular changes. One of the ablest administrative sea-officers, both afloat and ashore, that I have known in my professional career, stated before a Congressional committee that he had "always believed it would be wise to have a board of five officers for the purpose of harmonizing difficulties between bureaus, settling upon a ship-building policy, and other matters that embarrass the head of the Department on account of a lack of professional knowledge." I do not undertake to pass an opinion upon this particular suggestion, but confine myself to remarking that the fault in the system certainly exists, and that any remedy requires the careful observance of two points: 1, that the adviser, one or a board, be wholly clear of administrative activity; and, 2, that he or they be advisers only, pure and simple, with no power to affect the individual responsibility of decision. This must be preserved under whatever method, as the Secretary's privilege as well as his obligation.

CHAPTER TWO

Globalization and the Fleet

At the start of the twentieth century most of Alfred Thayer Mahan's writing had been published in books. However, in the second half of 1901 he began contributing articles to the British magazine *National Review*. The articles were well received, both in Great Britain and the United States where *Review* editor Leopold Maxse circulated them. In 1903 Mahan took the first five articles that he wrote for that magazine and combined them with a handful of others from American magazines like *McClure's*, and published the collection of essays entitled *Retrospect and Prospect: Studies in International Relations, Naval and Political*.

One of the essays suggested by Maxse, when he and Mahan first corresponded over the idea of a series for *National Review*, was about "the strategic distribution of British Squadrons."[1]

"Considerations" opens with what Mahan called "an antecedent appreciation of the political, commercial, and military exigencies of the State." He felt it was important to first talk about the condition and political state of the world because the use and deployment of a fleet in peacetime should be done in anticipation of the needs of war. Mahan believed that any military policy had to be in tune with political and economic realities. This opening discussion centers around what readers in the twenty-first century may recognize as globalization.

The adoption of steam power, transatlantic telegraph cables, and wireless telegraph technology had dramatically shortened the connections around the world. This created a global economic and political system that Mahan referred to as "an articulated whole."[2] He foresaw that as commerce and economic considerations increased in power, there would be a desire to maintain the global status quo for reasons of economic power. The economic, political, and military power of a nation, according to Mahan, was all intertwined, and he wrote, "This is the more necessary to observe, because, while commerce thus on the one hand deters from war, on the other hand it engenders conflict, fostering ambitions and strifes which tend towards armed collision."[3] Mahan saw navies as the central players in any future armed conflict that was sparked by commercial competition in the entwined global system.

The article continues by discussing the state of naval deployments at the turn of the century. A general layout of the world's maritime interests leads him to a discussion of the roles of offense and defense in naval strategy and warfare. The United States, throughout the nineteenth century, had a very defensive naval policy, but Mahan felt that ensuring that America's fighting was done overseas was the safest course for the country. Such a strategy required a navy that could go on the offensive in order to defend the nation. This belief caused him to declare "the fundamental principles of all naval war, namely, that defence is insured only by offence."[4]

Following his discussion of the role of offense and defense in naval warfare, Mahan turns the article toward the question of what ships a fleet required and how they should be deployed. His discussion may surprise many students of naval affairs who have been taught that Mahan was strictly a battleship proponent. He lays out the need for a balanced fleet built around the foundation of the battlefleet, made up primarily of battleships, but also including small combatants that could serve as scouts and two distinct types of cruisers for the differing missions of working with the battle fleet and sailing independently in the protection of commerce. His discussion includes some ideas on the new technology of the wireless telegraph, and suggestions that read like opening thoughts on the naval uses of a networked battlefield. He writes about the idea that by using their radios, the ships could network together and be able to cover much larger distances, and that small ships could use the network to come together and fight as a unit when needed. Granted, this would be in order to support the larger battlefleet's operations, but it still offers the twenty-first century reader a glimpse of Mahan as appreciative of technological advancements.

Mahan looked outward from the United States and used the Royal Navy as an example to study the need for a navy that can deploy globally. He recognized the importance of operating forward, and of obtaining bases that can support a fleet or squadron's operations far from home. He reminded us that "he who has but half way to go does double the work,"[5] and he discussed the importance of maintaining naval facilities, or allies, for the repair and resupply of vessels while they are deployed. Having these facilities located in a central position, where the fleet can access them as needed without giving up geographical positions, is a key to success.

The essay offers a great deal for twenty-first century students of naval affairs. Mahan's view of the uniquely maritime aspects of offense and defense are interesting to read and compare to the work of Karl von Clausewitz and his view of land warfare. The discussion of a balanced fleet offers a different perspective on Mahan's thoughts than most students are accustomed to reading. As the fleets of traditional naval powers like the United States and Great Britain continue to shrink at the start of the new century, Mahan's thoughts on forward deployment and the vital nature of maintenance facilities to keep forces at sea are also worth consideration. In "Considerations Governing the Disposition of Navies," today's readers will find a number of tenets of naval warfare that have not changed despite the steady march of technology and the introduction of new weapons. These tenets can be applied to naval operations at the start of the twenty-first century just as they were at the beginning of the twentieth.

CONSIDERATIONS GOVERNING THE DISPOSITION OF NAVIES

May 1902

We have the highest military authority for saying that "War is a business of positions"; a definition which includes necessarily not only the selection of positions to be taken, with the reasonings, or necessities, which dictate the choice, but further also the assignment of proportionate force to the several points occupied. All this is embraced in the easy phrase, "The distribution of the fleet." In these words, therefore, ought to be involved, by necessary implication, an antecedent appreciation of the political, commercial, and military exigencies of the State in the event of possible wars; for the dispositions of peace should bear a close relation to the contingency of war. All three elements form a part of the subject-matter for consideration, for each is an essential factor in national life. Logically separable, in practice the political, commercial, and military needs are so intertwined that their mutual interaction constitutes one problem. The frequent statement that generals in the field have no account to take of political considerations, conveys, along with a partial truth, a most misleading inference. Applied even to military and naval leaders, it errs by lack of qualification; but for the statesman, under whom the soldier or seaman acts, the political as well as the military conditions must influence, must at times control, and even reverse, decision.

The choice of situations, localities, to be held as bases of operations, is governed by considerations of geographical position, military strength, and natural resources, which endure from age to age; a permanence which justifies the expense of adequate fortification. The distribution of mobile force, military or naval, is subject to greater variation, owing to changes of circumstances. Nevertheless, at any one historical moment, of peace or war, this question also admits of an appropriate fixed determination, general in outline, but not therefore necessarily vague. This conclusion should be the outcome of weighing the possible dangers of the State, and all the various factors—political, commercial, and military—which affect national welfare. The disposition thence adopted should be the one which will best expedite the several readjustments and combinations that may be necessitated by the outbreak of various particular wars, which may happen with this or that possible enemy. Such modification of arrangements can be predicated with reasonable certainty for a measurable period in advance. The decision thus reached may be called the "strategic" solution, because dependent upon ascertainable factors, relatively permanent, of all which it takes account; and because also it is accepted, consciously and of purpose, as preliminary to the probable great movements of war, present or prospective.

In the particular cases that afterwards arise from time to time, and of which the outbreak of war may itself be one, the unforeseen, the unexpected, begins to come into operation. This is one of the inevitable accompaniments of warfare. The meeting of these new conditions, by suitable changes of plan, is temporary in character, varying possibly from day to day; but it will generally be found that the more comprehensive has been the previous strategic study, and the more its just forecasts have controlled the primary disposition—the distribution of force—the more certainly and readily will this lend itself to the shifting incidents of hostilities. These movements bear to the fundamental general dispositions the relations which tactics have to strategy. In them, on occasions, one or two of the leading considerations which have each had their full weight in the original dispositions, may have to be momentarily subordinated to the more pressing demand of a third. In war, generally and naturally, military exigencies have preponderant weight; but even in war the safety of a great convoy, or of a commercial strategic centre, may at a given instant be of more consequence than a particular military gain. So political conditions may rightly be allowed at times to overweigh military prudence, or to control military activity. This is eminently true, for, after all, war is political action. The old phrase, "The cannon is the last argument of kings," may now be paraphrased, "War is the last argument of diplomacy." Its purpose is to compass political results, where peaceful methods have failed; and while undoubtedly, as war, the game should be played in accordance with the well-established principles of the art, yet, as a means to an end, it must consent to momentary modifications, in accepting which a well-balanced mind admits that the means are less than the end, and must be subjected to it.

The question between military and political considerations is therefore one of proportion, varying from time to time as attendant circumstances change. As regards the commercial factor, never before in the history of the world has it been so inextricably commingled with politics. The interdependence of nations for the necessities and luxuries of life have been marvelously increased by the growth of population and the habits of comfort contracted by the peoples of Europe and America through a century of comparative peace, broken only by wars which, though gigantic in scale, have been too short in duration to affect seriously commercial relations. The unmolested course of commerce, reacting upon itself, has contributed also to its own rapid development, a result furthered by the prevalence of a purely economical conception of national greatness during the larger part of the century. This, with the vast increase in rapidity of communication, has multiplied and strengthened the bonds knitting the interests of nations to one another, till the whole now forms an articulated system, not only of prodigious size and activity, but of an excessive sensitiveness, unequalled in former ages. National nerves are exasperated by the delicacy of financial situations, and national resistance to hardship is sapped by generations that have known war only by the battlefield, not in the prolonged endurance of privation and straitness extending through years and reaching every class of the community. The preservation of commercial and financial interests constitutes now a political consideration of the first importance, making for peace and deterring from war; a fact well worthy of observation by those who would exempt maritime commercial intercourse from the operations of naval war, under the illusory plea of protecting private property at sea. Ships and cargoes in transit upon the sea are private property in only one point of view, and that the narrowest. Internationally considered, they are national wealth engaged in reproducing and multiplying itself, to the intensification of the national power, and that by the most effective process; for it relieves the nation from feeding upon itself, and makes the whole outer world contribute to its support. It is therefore a most proper object of attack; more humane, and more conducive to the objects of war, than the slaughter of men. A great check on war would be removed by assuring immunity to a nation's seaborne trade, the life-blood of its power, the assurer of its credit, the purveyor of its comfort.

This is the more necessary to observe, because, while commerce thus on the one hand deters from war, on the other hand it engenders conflict, fostering ambitions and strifes which tend towards armed collision. Thus it has continuously been from the beginning of sea power. A conspicuous instance was afforded by the Anglo-Dutch wars of the seventeenth century. There were other causes of dissatisfaction between the two nations, but commercial jealousies, rivalry for the opening markets of the newly discovered hemispheres, and for the carrying trade of the world, was the underlying national, as distinguished from the purely governmental motive, which inspired the fierce struggle. Blood was indeed shed, in profusion; but it was the suppression of maritime commerce that caused the grass to grow in the streets of Amsterdam, and brought the Dutch Republic to its knees. This too, it was, that sapped the vital force of Napoleon's Empire, despite the huge tributes exacted by him from the conquered states of Europe, external to his own dominions. The commerce of our day has brought up children, nourished populations, which now turn upon the mother, crying for bread. "The place is too strait for us; give place where we can sell more." The provision of markets for the production of an ever-increasing number of inhabitants is a leading political problem of the day, the solution of which is sought by methods commercial and methods political, so essentially combative, so offensive and defensive in character, that direct military action would be only a development of them, a direct consequent; not a breach of continuity in spirit, however it might be in form. As the interaction of commerce and finance shows a unity in the modern civilized world, so does the struggle for new markets and for predominance in old, reveal the unsubdued diversity. Here every state is for itself; and in every great state the look for the desired object is outward, just as it was in the days when England and Holland fought over the Spice Islands and the other worlds newly opening before them. Beyond the seas, now as then, are to be found regions scantily populated where can be built up communities with wants to be supplied; while elsewhere are teeming populations who may be led or manipulated to recognize necessities of which they have before been ignorant, and stimulated to provide for them through a higher development of their resources, either by themselves, or, preferably, through the exploitation of foreigners.

We are yet but at the beginning of this marked movement, much as has been done in the way of partition and appropriation within the last twenty years. The regions—chiefly in Africa—which the Powers of Europe have divided by mutual consent, if not to mutual satisfaction, await the gradual process of utilization of their natural resources and consequent increase of inhabitants, the producers and consumers of a commerce yet to be in the distant future. The degree and rate of this development must depend upon the special aptitudes of the self-constituted owners, whose needs meantime are immediate. Their eyes therefore turn necessarily for the moment to quarters where the presence of a population already abundant provides at once, not only numerous buyers and sellers, but the raw material of labor, by which, under suitable direction and with foreign capital, the present production may be multiplied. It is not too much to say that, in order further to promote this commercial action, existing political tenure is being assailed; that the endeavor is to supplant it, as hindering the commercial, or possibly the purely military or political ambitions of the intruder. Commercial enterprise is never so secure, nor so untrammelled, as under its own flag; and when the present owner is obstructive by temperament, as China is, the impulse to overbear its political action by display of force tends to become ungovernable. At all events the fact is notorious; nor can it be seriously doubted that in several other parts of the globe aggression is only deterred by the avowed or understood policy of a powerful opponent, not by the strength of the present possessor. This is the significance of the new Anglo-Japanese agreement, and also of the more venerable Monroe Doctrine of the United States, though that is applicable in another quarter. The parties to either of these policies is interested in the success of the other.

It seems demonstrable, therefore, that as commerce is the engrossing and predominant interest of the world to-day, so, in consequence of its acquired expansion, oversea commerce, oversea political acquisition, and maritime commercial routes are now the primary objects of external policy among nations. The instrument for the maintenance of policy directed upon these objects is the Navy of the several States; for, whatever influence we attribute to moral ideas, which I have no wish to undervalue, it is certain that, while right rests upon them for its sanction, it depends upon force for adequate assertion against the too numerous, individuals or communities, who either disregard moral sanctions, or reason amiss concerning them.

Further, it is evident that for the moment neither South America nor Africa is an immediate object of far-reaching commercial ambition, to be compassed by political action. Whatever the future may have in store for them, a variety of incidents have relegated them for the time to a position of secondary interest. Attention has centred upon the Pacific generally, and upon the future of China particularly. The present distribution of navies indicates this; for while largely a matter of tradition and routine, nevertheless the assignment of force follows the changes of political circumstances, and undergoes gradual modifications, which reflect the conscious or unconscious sense of the nation that things are different. It is not insignificant that the preponderant French fleet is now in the Mediterranean, whereas it once was in the Atlantic ports; and memories which stretch a generation back can appreciate the fact and the meaning of the diminution of British force on the east and west coasts of America, as also of the increase of Russian battleship force in China seas. Interests have shifted.

Directly connected with these new centres of interest in the Far East, inseparable from them in fact or in policy, are the commercial routes which lead to them. For the commerce and navies of Europe this route is by the Mediterranean and the Suez Canal. This is the line of communication to the objective of interest. The base of all operation, political or military—so far as the two are separable—is in the mother countries. These—the base, the objective, and the communications—are the conditions of the problem by which the distribution of naval force is ultimately to be determined. It is to be remarked, however, that while the dominant factor of the three is the line of communication between base and objective, the precise point or section of this upon which control rests, and on which mobile force must be directed, is not necessarily always the same. The distribution of force must have regard to possible changes of dispositions, as the conditions of a war vary.

Every war has two aspects, the defensive and the offensive, to each of which there is a corresponding factor of activity. There is something to gain, the offensive; there is something to lose, the defensive. The ears of men, especially of the uninstructed, are more readily and sympathetically open to the demands of the latter. It appeals to the conservatism which is dominant in the well-to-do, and to the widespread timidity which hesitates to take any risk for the sake of a probable though uncertain gain.

The sentiment is entirely respectable in itself, and more than respectable when its power is exercised against breach of the peace for other than the gravest motives—for any mere lucre of gain. But its limitations must be understood. A sound defensive scheme, sustaining the bases of the national force, is the foundation upon which war rests; but who lays a foundation without intending a superstructure? The offensive element in warfare is the superstructure, the end and aim for which the defensive exists, and apart from which it is to all purposes of war worse than useless. When war has been accepted as necessary, success means nothing short of victory; and victory must be sought by offensive measures, and by them only can be insured. "Being in, bear it, that the opposer may be ware of thee." No mere defensive attitude or action avails to such end. Whatever the particular mode of offensive action adopted, whether it be direct military attack, or the national exhaustion of the opponent by cutting off the sources of national well-being, whatsoever method may be chosen, offence, injury, weakening of the foe, to annihilation if need be, must be the guiding purpose of the belligerent. Success will certainly attend him who drives his adversary into the position of the defensive and keeps him there.

Offence therefore dominates, but it does not exclude. The necessity for defence remains obligatory, though subordinate. The two are complementary. It is only in the reversal of *roles*, by which priority of importance is assigned to the defensive, that ultimate defeat is involved. Nor is this all. Though opposed in idea and separable in method of action, circumstances not infrequently have permitted the union of the two in a single general plan of campaign, which protects at the same time that it attacks. "Fitz James's blade was sword and shield." Of this the system of blockades by the British Navy during the Napoleonic wars was a marked example. Thrust up against the ports of France, and lining her coasts, they covered—shielded—the operations of their own commerce and cruisers in every sea; while at the same time, crossing swords, as it were, with the fleets within, ever on guard, ready to attack, should the enemy give an opening by quitting the shelter of his ports, they frustrated his efforts at a combination of his squadrons by which alone he could hope to reverse conditions. All this was defensive; but the same operation cut the sinews of the enemy's power by depriving him of sea-borne commerce, and promoted the reduction of his colonies. Both these were measures of offence; and both, it may be added, were directed upon the national communications, the sources of national well-being. The means was one, the effect two-fold.

It is evident also that offensive action depends for energy upon the security of the several places whence its resources are drawn. These are appropriately called "bases," for they are the foundations—more exactly, perhaps, the roots—severed from which vigor yields to paralysis. Still more immediately disastrous would be the destruction or capture of the base itself. Therefore, whether it be the home country in general, the centre of the national power, or the narrower localities where are concentrated the materials of warfare in a particular region, the base, by its need of protection, represents distinctively the defensive element in any campaign. It must be secured at all hazards; though, at the same time, be it clearly said, by recourse to means which shall least fetter the movements of the offensive factor—the mobile force, army or navy. On the other hand, the objective represents with at least equal exclusiveness the offensive element; there, put it at the least, preponderance over the enemy, not yet existent, is to be established by force. The mere effort to get from the base to the objective is an offensive movement; but the ground intervening between the two is of more complex character. Here, on the line of communications, offence and defence blend. Here the belligerent whose precautions secure suitable permanent positions, the defensive element, and to them assign proportionate mobile force, the offensive factor, sufficient by superiority to overpower his opponent, maintains, by so far and insomuch, his freedom and power of action at the distant final objective; for he controls for his own use the indispensable artery through which the national life-blood courses to the distant fleet, and by the same act he closes it to his enemy. Thus again offence and defence meet, each contributing its due share of effect, unified in method and result by an accurate choice of the field of exertion, of that section of the line of communications where power needs to be mainly exerted.

In purely land warfare the relative strength of the opponents manifests itself in the length of the line of communications each permits itself; the distance, that is, which it ventures to advance from its base towards the enemy. The necessary aim of both is superiority at the point of contact, to be maintained either by actual preponderance of numbers, or else by a combination of inferior numbers with advantageous position. The original strength of each evidently affects the distance that he can thus advance, for the line of communication behind him must be secured by part of his forces, because upon it he depends for almost daily supplies. The weaker therefore can go least distance, and may even be compelled to remain behind the home frontier—a bare defensive—yielding the other the moral and material advantage of the offensive. But commonly, in land war, each adversary has his own line of communication, which is behind him with respect to his opponent; each being in a somewhat literal sense opposite, as well as opposed, to the other, and the common objective, to be held by the one or carried by the other, lying between them. The strategic aim of both is to menace, or even to sever permanently, the other's communications; for if they are immediately threatened he must retreat, and if sundered he must surrender. Either result is better obtained by this means than by the resort to fighting, for it saves bloodshed, and therefore economizes power for the purpose of further progress.

Maritime war has its analogy to these conditions, but it ordinarily reproduces them with a modification peculiar to itself. In it the belligerents are not usually on opposite sides of the common objective—though they may be so—but proceed towards it by lines that in general direction are parallel, or convergent, and may even be identical. England and France lie side by side, and have waged many maritime wars; but while there have been exceptions, as Gibraltar and Minorca, or when the command of the Channel was in dispute, the general rule has been that the scene of operations was far distant from both, and that both have approached it by substantially the same route. When the prospective theatre of war is reached, the fleet there depends partly upon secondary local bases of supplies, but ultimately upon the home country, which has continually to renew the local deposits, sending stores forward from time to time over the same paths that the fleets themselves travelled. The security of those sea-roads is therefore essential and the dependence of the fleets upon them for supplies of every kind—pre-eminently of coal—reproduces the land problem of communications in a specialized form. The two have to contest the one line of communications vital to both. It becomes therefore itself an objective, and all the more important because the security of military communications entails in equal measure that of the nation's commerce. In broad generalization, the maritime line of communications is the ocean itself, an open plain, limited by no necessary highways, such as the land has to redeem from the obstacles which encumber it, and largely devoid of the advantages of position that the conformation of ground may afford in a shore battlefield. In so far control depends upon superior numbers only, and the give and take which history records, where disparity has not been great, has gone far to falsify the frequent assertion that the ocean acknowledges but one mistress; but as the sea-road draws near a coast, the armed vessels that assail or protect are facilitated in their task if the shore affords them harbors of refuge and supply. A ship that has to go but fifty miles to reach her field of operation will do in the course of a year the work of several ships that have to go five hundred. Fortified naval depots at suitable points therefore increase numerical force by multiplying it, quite as the possession of strategic points, or the lay of the ground of a battlefield, supply numerical deficiencies.

Hence appears the singular strategic—and, because strategic, commercial—interest of a narrow or landlocked sea, which is multiplied manifold when it forms an essential link in an important maritime route. Many widely divergent tracks may be traced on the ocean's unwrinkled brow; but specifically the one military line of communications between any two points of its surface is that which is decisively the shortest. The measure of force between opponents in such a case depends therefore not only upon superiority at the objective point, but upon control of that particular line of communications; for so only can superiority be maintained. The belligerent who, for any disadvantage of numbers, or from inferiority of strength as contrasted with the combined numbers and position of his opponent, cannot sustain his dominant hold there is already worsted.

To this consideration is due the supreme importance of the Mediterranean in the present conditions of the communications and policies of the world. From the commercial point of view it is much the shortest, and therefore the principal, sea route between Europe and the Farther East. At the present time very nearly one-third of the home trade, the exports and imports, of Great Britain originates in or passes through the Mediterranean; and the single port of Marseilles handles a similar proportion of all the sea-borne commerce of France. From the military standpoint, the same fact of shortness, combined with the number and rivalry of national tenures established throughout its area, constitutes it the most vital and critical link in an interior line between two regions of the gravest international concern. In one of these, in Europe, are situated the bases, the home dominions, of the European Powers concerned, and in the other the present chief objective of external interest to all nations of to-day—that Farther East and western Pacific upon which so many events have conspired recently to fasten the anxious attention of the world.

The Mediterranean therefore becomes necessarily the centre around which must revolve the strategic distribution of European navies. It does not follow, indeed, that the distribution of peace reproduces the dispositions for war; but it must look to them, and rest upon the comprehension of them. The decisive point of action in case of war must be recognized and preparation made accordingly; not only by the establishment of suitable positions, which is the naval strategy of peace, but by a distinct relation settled between the numbers and distribution of vessels needed in war and those maintained in peace. The Mediterranean will be either the seat of one dominant control, reaching thence in all directions, owning a single mistress, or it will be the scene of continual struggle. Here offence and defence will meet and blend in their general manifestation of mobile force and fortified stations. Elsewhere the one or the other will have its distinct sphere of predominance. The home waters and their approaches will be the scene of national defence in the strictest and most exclusive sense; but it will be defence that exists for the foundation, upon which reposes the struggle for, or the control of, the Mediterranean. The distant East, in whatever spot there hostilities may rage, will represent, will be, the offensive sphere; but the determination of the result, in case of prolongation of war, will depend upon control of the Mediterranean. In the degree to which that is insured defence will find the test of its adequacy, and offence the measure of its efficiency.

In this combination of the offensive and defensive factors the Mediterranean presents an analogy to the military conditions of insular states, such as Great Britain and Japan, in which the problem of national defence becomes closely identified with offensive action. Security, which is simply defence in its completed result, depends for them upon control of the sea, which can be assured only by the offensive action of the national fleet. Its predominance over that of the enemy is sword and shield. It is a singular advantage to have the national policy in the matter of military development and dispositions so far simplified and unified as it is by this consideration. It much more than compensates for the double line of communications open to a continental state, the two strings to its bow, by its double frontiers of sea and land; for with the two frontiers there is double exposure as well as double utility. They require two-fold protective action, dissipating the energies of the nation by dividing them between two distinct objects, to the injury of both.

An insular state, which alone can be purely maritime, therefore contemplates war from a position of antecedent probable superiority from the two-fold concentration of its policy; defence and offence being closely identified, and energy, if exerted judiciously, being fixed upon the increase of naval force to the clear subordination of that more narrowly styled military. The conditions tend to minimize the division of effort between offensive and defensive purpose, and, by greater comparative development of the fleet, to supply a larger margin of disposable numbers in order to constitute a mobile superiority at a particular point of the general field. Such a decisive local superiority at the critical point of action is the chief end of the military art, alike in tactics and strategy. Hence it is clear that an insular state, if attentive to the conditions that should dictate its policy, is inevitably led to possess a superiority in that particular kind of force, the mobility of which enables it most readily to project its power to the more distant quarters of the earth, and also to change its point of application at will with unequalled rapidity.

The general considerations that have been advanced concern all the great European nations, in so far as they look outside their own continent, and to maritime expansion, for the extension of national influence and power; but the effect upon the action of each differs necessarily according to their several conditions. The problem of sea-defence, for instance, relates primarily to the protection of the national commerce everywhere, and specifically as it draws near the home ports; serious attack upon the coast, or upon the ports themselves, being a secondary consideration, because little likely to befall a nation able to extend its power far enough to sea to protect its merchant ships. From this point of view the position of Germany is embarrassed at once by the fact that she has, as regards the world at large, but one coast-line. To and from this all her sea commerce must go; either passing the English Channel, flanked for three hundred miles by France on the one side and England on the other, or else going north about by the Orkneys, a most inconvenient circuit, and obtaining but imperfect shelter from recourse to this deflected route. Holland, in her ancient wars with England, when the two were fairly matched in point of numbers, had dire experience of this false position, though her navy was little inferior in numbers to that of her opponent. This is another exemplification of the truth that distance is a factor equivalent to a certain number of ships. Sea-defence for Germany, in case of war with France or England, means established naval pre-dominance at least in the North Sea; nor can it be considered complete unless extended through the Channel and as far as Great Britain will have to project hers into the Atlantic. This is Germany's initial disadvantage of position, to be overcome only by adequate superiority of numbers; and it receives little compensation from the security of her Baltic trade, and the facility for closing that sea to her enemies. In fact, Great Britain, whose North Sea trade is but one-fourth of her total, lies to Germany as Ireland does to Great Britain, flanking both routes to the Atlantic; but the great development of the British seacoast, its numerous ports and ample internal communications, strengthen that element of sea-defence which consists in abundant access to harbors of refuge.

For the Baltic Powers, which comprise all the maritime States east of Germany, the commercial drawback of the Orkney route is a little less than for Hamburg and Bremen, in that the exit from the Baltic is nearly equidistant from the north and south extremities of England; nevertheless the excess in distance over the Channel route remains very considerable. The initial naval disadvantage is in no way diminished. For all the communities east of the Straits of Dover it remains true that in war commerce is paralyzed, and all the resultant consequences of impaired national strength entailed, unless decisive control of the North Sea is established. That effected, there is security for commerce by the northern passage; but this alone is mere defence. Offence, exerted anywhere on the globe, requires a surplusage of force, over that required to hold the North Sea, sufficient to extend and maintain itself west of the British Islands. In case of war with either of the Channel Powers, this means, as between the two opponents, that the eastern belligerent has to guard a long line of communications, and maintain distant positions, against an antagonist resting on a central position, with interior lines, able to strike at choice at either wing of the enemy's extended front. The relation which the English Channel, with its branch the Irish Sea, bears to the North Sea and the Atlantic—that of an interior position—is the same which the Mediterranean bears to the Atlantic and the Indian Sea; nor is it merely fanciful to trace in the passage round the north of Scotland an analogy to that by the Cape of Good Hope. It is a reproduction in miniature. The conditions are similar, the scale different. What the one is to a war whose scene is the north of Europe, the other is to operations by European Powers in Eastern Asia.

To protract such a situation is intolerable to the purse and *morale* of the belligerent who has the disadvantage of position. This of course leads us straight back to the fundamental principles of all naval war, namely, that defence is insured only by offence, and that the one decisive objective of the offensive is the enemy's organized force, his battle-fleet. Therefore, in the event of a war between one of the Channel Powers, and one or more of those to the eastward, the control of the North Sea must be at once decided. For the eastern State it is a matter of obvious immediate necessity, of commercial self-preservation. For the western State the offensive motive is equally imperative; but for Great Britain there is defensive need as well. Her Empire imposes such a development of naval force as makes it economically impracticable to maintain an army as large as those of the Continent. Security against invasion depends therefore upon the fleet. Postponing more distant interests, she must here concentrate an indisputable superiority. It is, however, inconceivable that against any one Power Great Britain should not be able here to exert from the first a preponderance which would effectually cover all her remoter possessions. Only an economical decadence, which would of itself destroy her position among nations, could bring her so to forego the initial advantage she has, in the fact that for her offence and defence meet and are fulfilled in one factor, the command of the sea. History has conclusively demonstrated the inability of a state with even a single continental frontier to compete in naval development with one that is insular, although of smaller population and resources. A coalition of Powers may indeed affect the balance. As a rule, however, a single state against a coalition holds the interior position, the concentrated force; and while calculation should rightly take account of possibilities, it should beware of permitting imagination too free sway in presenting its pictures. Were the eastern Powers to combine they might prevent Great Britain's use of the North Sea for the safe passage of her merchant shipping; but even so she would but lose commercially the whole of a trade, the greater part of which disappears by the mere fact of war. Invasion is not possible, unless her fleet can be wholly disabled from appearing in that sea. From her geographical position, she still holds her gates open to the outer world, which maintains three-fourths of her commerce in peace.

As Great Britain, however, turns her eyes from the North and Baltic Seas, which in respect to her relations to the world at large may justly be called her rear, she finds conditions confronting her similar to those which position entails upon her eastern neighbors. Here, however, a comparison is to be made. The North Sea is small, its coast-line contracted, the entrance to the Baltic a mere strait. Naval preponderance once established, the lines of transit, especially where they draw near the land, are easily watched. Doubtless, access to the British Islands from the Atlantic, if less confined by geographical surroundings, is constricted by the very necessity of approaching at all; but a preponderant fleet maintained by Great Britain to the south-west, in the prolongation of the Channel, will not only secure merchant shipping within its own cruising ground, but can extend its support by outlying cruisers over a great area in every direction. A fleet thus in local superiority imposes upon cruisers from the nearest possible enemy—France—a long circuit to reach the northern approaches of the islands, where they will arrive more or less depleted of coal, and in danger from ships of their own class resting on the nearer ports of Scotland or Ireland. Superiority in numbers is here again counterbalanced by advantage of position. Vessels of any other country, south or east, are evidently under still greater drawbacks.

As all the Atlantic routes and Mediterranean trade converge upon the Channel, this must be, as it always has been, among the most important stations of the British Navy. In the general scheme its office is essentially defence. It protects the economical processes which sustain national endurance, and thus secures the foundation on which the vigor of war rests. But its scope must be sanely conceived. Imaginative expectation and imaginative alarms must equally be avoided; for both tend to exaggerate the development of defensive dispositions at the expense of offensive power. Entire immunity for commerce must not be anticipated, nor should an occasional severe blow be allowed to force from panic concessions which calm reason rejects. Inconvenience and injury are to be expected, and must be borne in order that the grasp upon the determining points of war may not be relaxed. It will be the natural policy of an enemy to intensify anxiety about the Channel, to retain or divert thither force which were better placed elsewhere. By the size of her navy and by her geographical situation France is the most formidable maritime enemy of Great Britain, and therefore supplies the test to which British dispositions must be brought; but it is probable that in war, as now in peace, France must keep the larger part of her fleet in the Mediterranean. Since the days of Napoleon she has given hostages to fortune in the acquisition of her possessions on the African continent and beyond Suez. Her position in the Mediterranean has become to her not only a matter of national sentiment, which it long has been, but a question of military importance much greater than when Corsica was all she owned there. It is most unlikely that Brest and Cherbourg combined will in our day regain the relative importance of the former alone, a century ago.

In view of this, and barring the case of a coalition, I conceive that the battle-ships of the British Channel Fleet would not need to outnumber those of France in the near waters by more than enough to keep actually at sea a force equal to hers. A surplus for reliefs would constitute a reserve for superiority; that is all. The great preponderance required is in the cruisers, who are covered in their operations by the battle-fleet; the mere presence of the latter with an adequate scouting system secures them from molestation. Two classes of cruisers are needed, with distinct functions; those which protect commerce by the strong hand and constant movement, and those that keep the battle-fleet informed of the enemy's actions. It is clear that the close watching of hostile ports, an operation strictly tactical, has undergone marked changes of conditions since the old days. The ability to go to sea and steer any course under any conditions of wind, and the possibilities of the torpedo-boat, exaggerated though these probably have been in anticipation, are the two most decisive new factors. To them are to be added the range of coast guns, which keeps scouts at a much greater distance than formerly, and the impossibility now of detecting intentions which once might be inferred from the conditions of masts and sails.

On the other hand the sphere of effectiveness has been immensely increased for the scout by the power to move at will, and latterly by the wireless telegraphy. With high speed and large numbers, it should be possible to sweep the surroundings of any port so thoroughly as to make the chance of undetected escape very small, while the transmission of the essential facts—the enemy's force and the direction taken—is even more certain than detection. A lookout ship to-day will not see an enemy going off south with a fresh fair breeze, which is for herself a head wind to reach her own fleet a hundred miles to the northward. She may not need even to steam to the main body; but, telephoning the news, she will seek to keep the enemy in sight, gathering round her for the same work all of her own class within reach of her electric voice. True, an enemy may double on his track, or otherwise ultimately elude; but the test so imposed on military sagacity and inference is no greater than it formerly was. The data are different; the problem of the same class. Where can he go fruitfully? A raid? Well, a raid, above all a maritime raid, is only a raid; a black eye, if you will, but not a bullet in the heart, nor yet a broken leg. To join another fleet? That is sound, and demands action; but the British battle-fleet having immediate notice, and a fair probability of more information, should not be long behind. There is at all events no perplexity exceeding that with which men of former times dealt successfully. In the same way, and by the same methods, it should be possible to cover an extensive circumference to seaward so effectively that a merchant vessel reaching any point thereof would be substantially secure up to the home port.

The battle-fleet would be the tactical centre upon which both systems of scouts would rest. To close-watch a port to-day requires vessels swifter than the battle-ships within, and stronger in the aggregate than their cruiser force. The former then cannot overtake to capture, nor outrun to elude; and the latter, which may overtake, cannot drive off their post, nor successfully fight, because inferior in strength. Add to the qualities thus defined sufficient numbers to watch by night the arc of a circle of five miles radius, of which the port is the centre, and you have dispositions extremely effective against an enemy's getting away unperceived. The vessels nearest in are individually so small that the loss of one by torpedo is militarily immaterial; moreover, the chances will by no means all be with the torpedo-boat. The battle-fleet, a hundred or two miles distant it may be, and in a different position every night, is as safe from torpedo attack as ingenuity can place it. Between it and the inside scouts are the armored cruisers, faster than the hostile battle-fleet, stronger than the hostile cruisers. These are tactical dispositions fit for to-day; and in essence they reproduce those of St. Vincent before Brest, and his placing of Nelson at Cadiz with an inshore squadron, a century ago. "A squadron of frigates and cutters plying day and night in the opening of the Goulet; five ships-of-the-line anchored about ten miles outside; and outside of them again three of-the-line under sail." The main body, the battle-fleet of that time, was from twenty five to forty miles distant—the equivalent in time of not less than a hundred miles to-day.

Keeping in consideration these same waters, the office and function of the Channel Fleet may be better realized by regarding the battleships as the centre, from which depart the dispositions for watching, not only the enemy's port, but also the huge area to seaward which it is desired to patrol efficiently for the security of the national commerce. Take a radius of two hundred miles; to it corresponds a semicircle of six hundred, all within Marconi range of the centre. The battle-fleet never separates. On the far circumference move the lighter and swifter cruisers; those least able to resist, if surprised by an enemy, but also the best able to escape, and the loss of one of which is inconsiderable, as of the inner cruisers off the port. Between them and the fleet are the heavier cruisers, somewhat dispersed, in very open order, but in mutual touch, with a squadron organization and a plan of concentration, if by mischance an enemy's division come upon one of them unawares. Let us suppose, under such a danger, they are one hundred miles from the central body. It moves out at twelve miles an hour, they in at fifteen. Within four hours the force is united, save the light cruisers. These, as in all ages, must in large measure look out for themselves, and can do so very well.

Granting, as required by the hypothesis, equality in battle-ships and a large preponderance in cruisers—not an unreasonable demand upon an insular state—it seems to me that for an essentially defensive function there is here a fairly reliable, systematized, working disposition. It provides a semi-circumference of six hundred miles, upon reaching any point of which a merchant ship is secure for the rest of her homeward journey. While maintained, the national frontier is by so much advanced, and the area of greatest exposure for the merchant fleet equally reduced. Outside this, cruising as formerly practised can extend very far a protection, which, if less in degree, is still considerable. For this purpose, in my own judgment, and I think by the verdict of history, dissociated single ships are less efficient than cruiser-squadrons, such as were illustrated by the deeds of Jean Bart and Pellew. One such, a half-dozen strong, west of Finisterre, and another west of Scotland, each under a competent chief authorized to move at discretion over a fairly wide area, beyond the bailiwick of the commander-in-chief, would keep enemies at a respectful distance from much more ground than he actually occupies; for it is to be remembered that the opponent's imagination of danger is as fruitful as one's own.

In conception, this scheme is purely defensive. Incidentally, if opportunity offer to injure the enemy it will of course be embraced, but the controlling object is to remove the danger to home commerce by neutralizing the enemy's fleet. To this end numbers and force are calculated. This done, the next step is to consider the Mediterranean from the obvious and inevitable military point of view that it is the one and only central position, the assured control of which gives an interior line of operations from the western coast of Europe to the eastern waters of Asia. To have assured safety to the home seas and seaboard is little, except as a means to further action; for, if to build without a foundation is disastrous, to lay foundations and not to be able to build is impotent, and that is the case where disproportioned care is given to mere defensive arrangements. The power secured and stored at home must be continually transmitted to the distant scene of operations, here assumed, on account of the known conditions of world politics, to be the western Pacific, which, under varying local designations, washes the shores of the Farther East.

It has been said that in the Mediterranean, as the principal link in the long chain of communications, defence and offence blend. Moreover, since control here means assured quickest transmission of reinforcements and supplies in either direction, it follows that, while preponderance in battle-ship force is essential in the Far East, where if war occurs the operations will be offensive, such predominance in the Mediterranean, equally essential in kind, must be much greater in degree. In fact, the offensive fleet in the Eastern Seas and the defensive fleet in the Channel are the two wings, or flanks, of a long front of operations, the due security of both of which depends upon the assured tenure of the central position. Naturally, therefore, the Mediterranean fleet, having to support both, possibly even to detach hurriedly to one or the other, has in itself that combination of defensive and offensive character which ordinarily inheres in sea communications as such.

If this assertion be accepted in general statement, it will be fortified by a brief consideration of permanent conditions; with which it is further essential to associate as present temporary factors the existing alliances between France and Russia, Great Britain and Japan. The Triple Alliance, of the renewal of which we are assured, does not contemplate among its objects any one that is directly affected by the control of the Mediterranean. Should an individual member engage in war having its scene there, it would be as a power untrammelled by this previous engagement.

History and physical conformation have constituted unique strategic conditions in the Mediterranean. To history is due the existing tenure of positions, the bases, of varying intrinsic value, and held with varying degrees of power and firmness by several nations in several quarters. To examine these minutely and weigh their respective values as an element of strategic effect would be indeed essential to the particular planning of a naval campaign, or to the proper determination of the distribution of naval force, with a view to the combinations open to one's self or the enemy; but a paper dealing with general conditions may leave such detailed considerations to those immediately concerned. It must be sufficient to note the eminently central position of Malta, the unique position of Gibraltar, and the excentric situation of Toulon relatively to the great trade route. By conformation the Mediterranean has, besides the artificial canal—the frailest and most doubtful part of the chain—at least three straits of the utmost decisive importance, because there is to them no alternative passage by which vessels can leave the sea, or move from one part of it to another. In the Caribbean Sea, which is a kind of Mediterranean, the multiplicity of islands and passages reduces many of them to inconsequence, and qualifies markedly the effect of even the most important; but, in the Mediterranean, the Dardanelles, Gibraltar, and the belt of water separating the toe of Italy from Cape Bon in Africa, constitute three points of transit which cannot be evaded. It is true that in the last the situation of the island of Sicily allows vessels to go on its either side; but the surrounding conditions are such that it is scarcely possible for a fleet to pass undetected by an adversary making due use of his scouts. These physical peculiarities, conjointly with the positions specified, are the permanent features, which must underlie and control all strategic plans of Mediterranean Powers, among whom Russia must be inferentially included.

Geographically, Great Britain is an intruder in the Mediterranean. Her presence there at all, in territorial tenure, is distinctively military.

This is witnessed also by the character of her particular possessions. Nowhere does the vital energy of sea power appear more conspicuously, as self-expansive and self-dependent. To its historical manifestation is due the acquisitions which make the strength of her present position; but, as in history, so now, sea power itself must continue to sustain that which it begat. The habitual distribution of the warships of the United Kingdom must provide for a decisive predominance here, upon occasion arising, over any probable combination of enemies. Such provision has to take account not only of the total force of hostile divisions within and without the Mediterranean, but of movements intended to transfer one or more from or to that sea from other scenes of operations. Prevention of these attempts is a question, not of numbers chiefly, but of position, of stations assigned, of distribution. Predominance, to be militarily effectual, means not only an aggregate superiority to the enemy united, but ability to frustrate, before accomplishment, concentrations which might give him a local superiority anywhere. This is a question of positions more even than of numbers. In the Mediterranean, as the great centre, these two factors must receive such mutual adjustment as shall outweigh the combination of them on the part of the adversary. Where one is defective the other must be increased. The need is the more emphatic when the nation itself is external and distant from the sea, while possible antagonists, as Russia and France, are territorially contiguous; for it can scarcely be expected that the Russian Black Sea fleet would not force its way through the Dardanelles upon urgent occasion.

Evidently, too, Japan cannot in the near future contribute directly to maintain Great Britain in the Mediterranean. On the contrary, the declarations of Russia and France make plain that, if war arise, Japan must be supported in the Far East by her ally against a coalition, the uncertain element of which is the force that France will feel able to spare from her scattered, exposed interests. Russia labors under no such distraction; her singleness of eye is shown by the fact that the more efficient, and by far the larger part, of her so called Baltic fleet is now in the waters of China. In numbers and force she has there a substantial naval equality with

Japan, but under a disadvantage of position like that of Great Britain in the Mediterranean, in being remote from the centre of her power, imperfectly based, as yet, upon local resources, and with home communications by the shortest route gravely uncertain. Under these circumstances the decided step she has taken in the reinforcement of her Eastern Navy, carries the political inference that she for the present means to seek her desired access to unfrozen waters in Eastern Asia, preferably to the Mediterranean or the Persian Gulf. Having in view local difficulties and antagonistic interests elsewhere, this conclusion was probably inevitable; but its evident acceptance is notable.

For Great Britain it is also most opportune; and this raises a further question, attractive to speculative minds, viz.: whether the Anglo Japanese agreement has had upon Russia a stimulating or a deterrent effect? If it has increased her determination to utilize her present advantages, as represented in Port Arthur and its railroad, it would be in the direct line of a sound British policy; for it fixes the reasonable satisfaction of Russia's indisputable needs in a region remote from the greater interests of Great Britain, yet where attempts at undue predominance will elicit the active resistance of many competitors, intent upon their own equally indisputable rights. The gathering of the eagles on the coasts of China is manifest to the dullest eye. But should the alliance have the contrary effect of checking Russian development in that direction, her irrepressible tendency to the sea is necessarily thrown upon a quarter—the Levant or Persia—more distinctly ominous, and where, in the last named at least, Great Britain would find no natural supporter, enlisted by similarity of interest. The concentration of Russian ships in the East, taken in connection with the general trend of events there, is, however, as clear an indication of policy as can well be given.

In connection with the substantial numerical equality of Japan and Russia is to be taken, as one of the ascertained existing conditions, instituted so recently as to have a possible political significance, the reorganization of the French divisions beyond Suez into a single command, and the numbers thereto assigned. It is not to be supposed that this new disposition has been adopted without consideration of the new combinations indicated by the Anglo-Japanese treaty. It may even be in direct consequence. The relative strengths of this extensive eastern command and of the French Mediterranean fleet should in close measure reflect the official consciousness of the general naval situation, and of the power of France to give support to her recognized ally; directly in the East, and indirectly by military influence exerted upon the Mediterranean. Supposing Great Britain, on the other hand, to have made provision for the defensive control of the approaches to her home ports, how will she, and how can she, assure the joint ascendency of herself and her ally in the Farther East, the scene of the offensive, and her own single preponderance in the Mediterranean, the main link in the communications? These are the two intricate factors for consideration, calling for plans and movements not primarily defensive but offensive in scope. For France and for Great Britain, as a party to an alliance, the question is urgent, "How far can I go, how much spare from the Mediterranean to the East? In assisting my ally there, unless I bring him predominance, or at least nearly an equality, I waste my substance, little helping him. If paralyzed in the Mediterranean, thrown on a mere defensive, my force in the East is practically cut off. Like a besieged garrison, it may endure till relieved; but the situation is critical while it lasts, and carries imminent possibilities of disaster."

In approaching a military subject of this character it is necessary first and for all to disabuse the mind of the idea that a scheme can be devised, a disposition imagined, by which all risk is eliminated. Such an attractive condition of absolute security, if realized, would eliminate all war along with its risks. A British distribution, most proper for the Mediterranean alone, may entail the danger that a hostile body may escape into the Atlantic, may unite with the Brest and Cherbourg divisions against the Channel Fleet, and overwhelm the latter. True; but imagination must work both ways. It may also be that the escape cannot but be known at Gibraltar, telegraphed to England, and the fleet warned betimes so that the reserve ships, which give it a superiority to either detachment of the enemy, might join, and that its scouts, stationed as previously suggested, would gain for it the two hours of time needed to deal decisively with one division before the other turns up. These probabilities, known to the enemy, affect his actions just as one's own risks move one's self. Listen to Nelson contemplating just this contingency. "If the Ferrol squadron joins the Toulon, they will much outnumber us, but in that case I shall never lose sight of them, and Pellew" (from before Ferrol) "will soon be after them." But he adds, confirmatory of the need of numerous scouts, then as now, "I at this moment want ten frigates or sloops, when I believe neither the Ferrol or Toulon squadron could escape me." By this, I understand, is clearly intimated that he could look out both ways, intercept the first comer, frustrate the junction, and beat them in detail. If not before the action, Pellew would arrive in time to repair Nelson's losses and restore equality. The change in modern conditions would favor the modern Pellew more than the adversary.

So again disturbing political possibilities must be reasonably viewed. It may be that the whole Continent not only dislikes Great Britain, but would willingly combine for her military destruction; and that, if war begin, such a combination may come to pass. It may be; but this at least is certain, that interest, not liking, will decide so grave a matter. In the calculation of final issues, of national expenditure, of profit and loss, of relative national predominance resulting from a supposed success, I incline to think that Imperial Federation will be a far less difficult achievement than framing such a coalition. If the two dual alliances, the mutual opposition of which is apparent, come to blows, Germany may see it to her interest to strike hands with Russia and France; but it seems to me it would be so much more her interest to let them exhaust themselves, to the relief of her two flanks, that I find it difficult to believe she would not herself so view the question. There is one qualifying consideration. Germany cannot but wish a modification in the effect exerted upon her maritime routes by the position of Great Britain, already noted. As geographical situation cannot be changed, the only modification possible is the decrease of Great Britain's power by the lessening of her fleet. But, grant that object gained by such coalition, what remains? A Channel dominated by the French Navy no longer checked by the British; whereas with the latter as an ally the Channel would be almost as safe as the Kiel canal. If this remark is sound, it is but an illustration of the choice of difficulties presented by attempts to change permanent conditions by artificial combinations. As a matter of fact, no single power in Europe, save possibly Russia, is individually so weighty as to see without apprehension the effective elimination of any one factor in the present balance of power. The combined position and numbers of Russia do give her a great defensive security in her present tenures.

Admitting the Mediterranean to be distinctively and pre-eminently the crucial feature in any strategic scheme that contemplates Europe and the Farther East as the chief factors of interest, the positions before enumerated, in conjunction with the relative forces of the fleets, constitute the initial strategic situation. Assuming, as is very possible, that the decisive predominance, local or general, desired by either party, does not yet exist, the attempt of each must be to reach some preponderance by playing the game of war; by such applied pressure or strategic movements as shall procure a decisive momentary preponderance in some quarter, the due use of which, by the injury done the enemy, shall establish a permanent and decisive superiority. This is the one object of war scientifically—or better, artistically—considered. The nation that begins with the stronger fleet should initiate some offensive action, with the object of compelling the enemy to fight. This the latter cannot do, unless already in adequate strength at some one point, except by undertaking to combine his divided forces so as to effect a concentration in some quarter. The movements necessary to accomplish this are the opportunity of the offensive, to strike the converging divisions before their junction gives the desired local superiority. Herein is the skill; herein also the chance, the unexpected, the risk, which the best authorities tell us are inseparable from war, and constitute much of its opportunity as of its danger.

How shall the superior fleet exercise the needed compulsion? Ships cannot invade territory, unless there be unprotected navigable rivers. The stronger navy therefore cannot carry war beyond the sea-coast, home to the heart of the enemy, unless indeed its nation in addition to controlling the sea, can transport an overpowering force of troops. Of this the Transvaal war offers an illustration. Possibly, a disabling blow to the British fleet by the navy of one of the great continental armies might present a somewhat similar instance; but when the British fleet is thus enfeebled, Great Britain will be exposed to the conditions which it must be her own first effort, with her supreme navy, to impose on an opponent. Under such circumstances, there will be no need for an enemy to land an invading host on British soil. The interception of commerce at a half-dozen of the principal ports will do the work as surely, if less directly. Similarly, while the British Navy is what it is, the destruction of an enemy's commerce, not only by scattered cruisers at sea, but by a systematized, coherent effort directed against his ports and coasts, both home and colonial, must be the means of inflicting such distress and loss as shall compel his fleet to fight; or, if it still refuse, shall sap endurance by suffering and extenuation.

To effect this requires a battle-fleet superior in the aggregate to the one immediately opposed to it by at least so many ships as shall suffice to allow a constant system of reliefs. The battle-fleet is the solid nucleus of power. From it radiates the system of cruisers by which the trade blockade is maintained in technical, and as far as may be, in actual, efficiency. In case of hostilities with France, for example, the blockade of a principal commercial port, like Havre or Marseille, may be sustained in local efficiency by cruisers; but the security of these, and consequently the maintenance of the blockade, will depend upon such proximity of the battle-fleet as will prevent the French divisions at Cherbourg, Brest, or Toulon, from attacking them, except at great risk of being compelled to an engagement which it is presumably the specific aim of the British fleet to force. "Not blockade but battle is my aim," said Nelson: "on the sea alone we hope to realize the hopes and expectations of our country." A successful battle in any one quarter clears up the whole situation; that is, in proportion to the results obtained. This qualification is always to be borne in mind by a victorious admiral; for the general relief to his nation will correspond to the use made by him of the particular advantage gained. More or fewer of his ships will be liberated from their previous tasks, and can reinforce the station where the most assured predominance is desired. This by our analysis is the Mediterranean.

History has more than once shown how severe a compulsion may be exerted over an extensive coast by proper dispositions. Where a formidable, though inferior, navy lies in the ports of the blockaded state, the position and management of the battle-fleet, on either side, is the critical military problem. The task of the cruisers is simple, if arduous; to keep near the port assigned them, to hold their ground against equals, to escape capture by superior force. The battle-fleet must be so placed as effectually to cover the cruisers from the enemy's fleet, without unduly exposing itself; above all to torpedo attack. It must be on hand, not only to fight, but to chase to advantage, to make strategic movements, perhaps extensive in range, at short notice. War is a business of positions. Its position, suitably chosen, by supporting the cruiser force, covers the approaches of the national commerce, and also maintains both the commercial blockade and the close watch of the military ports. It may be noted that the commercial blockade is offensive in design, to injure the enemy and compel him to fight, while the other specified functions of the vessels are defensive. We therefore have here again a combination of the two purposes in a single disposition.

For some time to come nations distinctively European must depend upon the Mediterranean as their principal military route to the Far East. In the present condition of the Siberian railroad, Russia shares this common lot. While the other States have no land route whatever, hers is still so imperfect as not to constitute a valid substitute. Moreover, whatever resources of moderate bulk may be locally accumulated—coal, provisions, ammunition, and stores of various kinds—reinforcements of vessels, or reliefs to ships disabled by service or in battle can go only by sea.

Guns beyond a certain calibre are in like case. Every consideration emphasizes the importance of the Mediterranean. To it the Red Sea is simply an annex, the military status of which will be determined by that of its greater neighbor, qualified in some measure by the tenure of Egypt and Aden.

On the farther side of the isthmus, the naval operations throughout Eastern seas will depend for sustained vigor upon contact militarily maintained with the Mediterranean, and through that with home. In these days of cables, the decisive importance of Malta to India, recognized by Nelson and his contemporaries, is affirmed with quadruple force of the sea in which Malta is perhaps the most conspicuously important naval position. Reinforcements sent by the Cape, whether west or east, can always be anticipated at either end of the road by the Power which holds the interior line.

As regards special dispositions for the Eastern seas, embracing under that name all from Suez to Japan, the same factors—numbers and position—dictate distribution. To a central position, if such there be, must be assigned numbers adequate to immediate superiority, in order to control commercial routes, and to operate against the enemy whose approximate force and position are known. Such assignment keeps in view, necessarily, the possibilities of receiving reinforcements from the Mediterranean, or having to send them to China. Ceylon, for example, if otherwise suitable, is nearly midway between Suez and Hong-Kong; in round numbers, 3000 miles from each. Such a position favors a force of battle-ships as an advanced squadron from the Mediterranean, and would be a provision against a mishap at the canal interrupting reinforcements eastward. Position, with its two functions of distance and resources; there is nothing more prominent than these in Napoleon's analysis of a military situation. Numbers go, as it were, without saying. Where the power was his he multiplied them; but he always remembered that position multiplies spontaneously. He who has but half-way to go does double work. This is the privilege of central position.

The question of the Eastern seas introduces naturally the consideration of what the great self-governing colonies can do, not only for their own immediate security, and that of their trade, but for the general fabric of Imperial naval action, in the coherence of which they will find far greater assurance than in merely local effort. The prime naval considerations for them are that the British Channel Fleet should adequately protect the commerce and shores of the British Islands, and that the Mediterranean Fleet should insure uninterrupted transit for trade and for reinforcements. These effected and maintained, there will be no danger to their territory; and little to their trade except from single cruisers, which will have a precarious subsistence as compared with their own, based upon large self-supporting political communities. Australasia, however, can undoubtedly supply a very important factor, that will go far to fortify the whole British position in the Far East. A continent in itself, with a thriving population, and willing, apparently, to contribute to the general naval welfare, let it frame its schemes and base its estimates on sound lines, both naval and imperial; naval, by allowing due weight to battle force; imperial, by contemplating the whole, and recognizing that local safety is not always best found in local precaution. There is a military sense, in which it is true that he who loses his life shall save it.

In the Eastern seas, Australia and China mark the extremities of two long lines, the junction of which is near India; let us say, for sake of specificness, Ceylon. They are offshoots, each, of one branch, the root of which under present conditions, is the English Channel, and the trunk the Mediterranean. Now it is the nature of extremities to be exposed. To this our feet, hands, and ears bear witness, as does the military aphorism about salients; but while local protection has its value in these several cases, the general vigor and sustenance of the organism as a whole is the truer dependence. To apply this simile: it appears to me that the waters from Suez eastward should be regarded as a military whole, vitally connected with the system to the westward, but liable to temporary interruption at the Canal, against which precaution must be had. This recognizes at once the usual dependence upon the Channel and the Mediterranean, and the coincident necessity of providing for independent existence on emergency. In the nature of things there must be a big detachment east of Suez; the chance of its being momentarily cut off there is not so bad as its being stalled on the other side, dependent on the Cape route to reach the scene. But for the same reason that the Mediterranean and Malta are strategically eminent, because central, (as is likewise the Channel with reference to the North Sea and Atlantic), the permanent strategic centre of the Eastern seas is not by position in China, nor yet in Australia. It is to be found rather at a point which, approximately equidistant from both, is also equidistant from the Mediterranean and the East. Permanent, I say; not as ignoring that the force which there finds its centre may have to remove, and long to remain, at one extremity or another of the many radii thence issuing, but because there it is best placed to move in the shortest time in any one of the several directions. That from the same centre it best protects the general commercial interests is evident from an examination of the maps and of commercial returns.

Whether the essential unity of scope in naval action east of Suez should receive recognition by embracing Australia, China, and India, under one general command, with local subordinates, is a question administrative as well as strategic. As military policy it has a good side; for commanders previously independent do not always accept ungrudgingly the intrusion of a superior because of emergency of war. Military sensitiveness cannot prudently be left out of calculations. There would be benefit also in emphasizing in public consciousness the essential unity of military considerations, which should dominate the dispositions of the fleet. Non-professional—and even military—minds need the habit of regarding local and general interests in their true relations and proportions. Unless such correct appreciation exist, it is hard to silence the clamor for a simple local security, which is apparent but not real, because founded on a subdivision and dissemination of force essentially contrary to sound military principle. What Australasia needs is not her petty fraction of the Imperial navy, a squadron assigned to her in perpetual presence, but an organization of naval force which constitutes a firm grasp of the universal naval situation. Thus danger is kept remote; but, if it should approach, there is insured within reaching distance an adequate force to repel it betimes. There may, however, be fairly demanded the guarantee for the fleet's action, in a development of local dock-yard facilities and other resources which shall insure its maintenance in full efficiency if it have to come.

In this essential principle other colonies should acquiesce. The essence of the matter is that local security does not necessarily, nor usually, depend upon the constant local presence of a protector, ship or squadron, but upon general dispositions. As was said to and of Rodney, "Unless men take the great line, as you do, and consider the King's whole dominions as under their care, the enemy must find us unprepared somewhere. It is impossible to have a superior fleet in every part."

It is impossible; and it is unnecessary, granting the aggregate superiority at which Great Britain now aims. In the question of the disposition of force three principal elements are distinguishable in the permanent factors which we classify under the general head of "position." These are, the recognition of central positions, of interior lines—which means, briefly, shorter lines—and provision of abundant local dock-yard equipment in its widest sense. These furnish the broad outline, the skeleton of the arrangement. They constitute, so to say, the qualitative result of the analysis which underlies the whole calculation. Add to it the quantitative estimate of the interests at stake, the dangers at hand, the advantages of position, in the several quarters, and you reach the assignment of numbers, which shall make the dry bones live with all the energy of flesh and blood in a healthy body; where each member is supported, not by a local congestion of vitality, but by the vigor of the central organs which circulate nourishment to each in proportion to its needs.

CHAPTER THREE

Training of Officers and Sailors

In 1873 a group of fifteen naval officers gathered in the department of physics and chemistry building on the yard at the U.S. Naval Academy to talk shop. Their initial discussions were about naval history and strategy, but the conversations quickly migrated toward naval policy and modern considerations, as well. The group of officers, ranging from senior commissioned officers to junior warrant officers, decided to name their organization. They called themselves the United States Naval Institute and began putting together the structure for a professional organization that has become the heart of innovation and thought for the U.S. Navy for more than a century.

Alfred Thayer Mahan was promoted to commander in 1872 and was on sea duty as the commanding officer of USS *Wasp* at the time of USNI's founding. However, he arrived in Annapolis as the new head of the gunnery department at the conclusion of his orders in *Wasp* and immediately became involved in the organization. The ideals of the founders, that the study of military history and the free exchange of ideas were central to success as naval officers, were music to the ears of a Civil War veteran who feared that the rapid advance of steam power was turning his fellow officers into scientists and engineers rather than warriors.

Mahan took over as the president of the Institute, and in 1878 it was suggested by Lt. Cdr. Allan Brown that USNI follow the example of a number of naval organizations in Europe and establish an essay contest. The leaders of the Institute agreed, and in 1879 the first "General Prize Essay Contest" was established. The subject of the contest that year was "naval education," and Mahan wrote an essay to be entered in the contest on the proper training of naval officers and men. His essay was selected for third place in the contest and, along with the two essays selected ahead of his, it was published in *The Record of the United States Naval Institute*, the forerunner of today's *Proceedings*. It was Mahan's first published piece of writing.

The majority of Mahan's essay examines the curriculum at the United States Naval Academy, which was the only source of commissioned officers at the time. The course of study in the 1870s, as it is today, was very heavily weighted toward engineering and the hard sciences. The rise of steam power, and advancements in gunnery and the use of torpedoes, convinced many in the service that future naval officers were best served by being made into engineers. Mahan vehemently disagreed, and he wrote in the opening paragraphs of his essay that

> I confess to a feeling of mingled impatience and bitterness when I hear the noble duties and requirements of a naval officer's career ignored, and an attempt made to substitute for them the wholly different aims and faculties of the servant of science. The comparatively small scale on which those duties are now performed, the fancied impossibility of a great war, the pitiful condition of efficiency into which the material of the navy has been allowed to fall, have all helped to blind our eyes to the magnificence of the war seaman's career.[1]

In Mahan's view, naval officers were better served by an education that focused more on the humanities. The most important education that a future officer could receive was an education that emphasized moral strength, because combat decisionmaking required a strong moral grounding. Study in the humanities—English, history, tactics, and foreign languages—would allow junior officers to begin to build a "breadth of thought and loftiness of spirit."[2] These, he believed, were vital to the development of the proper moral reasoning that would encourage good leadership. He focused on the subjects that he believed would help instill "control [of] self and others; fearlessness in responsibility and in danger; self reliance; promptitude in action; readiness of resource; calmness amid excitement."[3] He also emphasized practical education, and the importance of the training that midshipmen received when they got out of the classroom and spent time on training vessels, conducting infantry drill and working artillery batteries. He believed that a certain amount of engineering, particularly the basics of steam locomotion, mathematics, and the foundations of navigation, were necessary, but that they should be taught at a practical level rather than a specialist level.

The commander wrote that an exclusive focus on engineering and science instilled bad habits in the midshipmen that would make them poor officers once they were assigned to sea duty. He believed that instilling midshipmen with grounding only in engineering and science tended "to promote caution unduly; to substitute calculation for judgment; to create trust in formulas rather than in one's self."[4] These were the exact opposite habits of what he felt a combat leader required.

According to Mahan, good naval leadership and strategy was an art and not a science. In his book *Naval Strategy: Compared and Contrasted with the Principles and Practice of Military Operations on*

Land, published in 1911, Mahan compared naval officers to artists. He wrote that artists had to learn certain techniques, mediums, and skills, but that wasn't what made their artwork great. In the end, "art, out of materials which it finds about, creates new forms in endless variety," and artists take those foundation basics and then mix and match them based on inspiration and experience to create a masterpiece. He believed that by increasing focus on the humanities, it would help midshipmen understand that frequently there are no right answers to military questions of strategy or leadership.

"Naval Education" also contains some thoughts on the proper training of sailors, as well as officers. The need to instill a sense of purpose and duty in sailors, and to help them broaden their understanding of their service to their country, is a focus that runs parallel to Mahan's thoughts on officers. He also warns against treating sailors like children, instead of the professional mariners that they are, warning of junior sailors: "no keeping them as children under special evident care. . . . In a word, if being the commander or first lieutenant you wish to look out for them, don't let it be by making a special class of them, whether for care or indulgence."[5]

In the twenty-first century the curriculum at the Naval Academy focuses heavily on engineering. As the technical requirements of enlisted sailors have increased, their general knowledge of naval history and pride in their heritage has also begun to diminish. Mahan warns against these tendencies. His ideas in "Naval Education" are as broadly valid today as they were almost a century and a half ago when he wrote them. Mahan's thinking and writing stretches well beyond naval strategy, the proper construction of battleships, and the importance of forward basing. The thoughts on leadership and training in the following essay can help add to modern views of the naval service, as well.

NAVAL EDUCATION.

"Essayons."

In considering the question of Naval Education for officers and men it is necessary to put clearly before us two things—1st, the material upon which we shall have to begin; 2d, what it is that we wish to make out of that material.

I. Officers.

In the case of officers the material will probably continue to be lads of from fourteen to seventeen years of age. The attainments of those lads at the time they come into the hands of their Naval educators will vary greatly. I am myself in favor of what is called a low standard for admission to the naval course, for two reasons. First, I think there is rough, substantial justice in the view that where Government provides an education out of the money of the whole people, the entrance upon that education should be, as far as possible, open to all parts of the country; as well to youths coming from less favored sections as to those whose homes are within reach of the best educational facilities. It may seem that the same argument would apply to a reduction of the final standard, or that of the whole course; but, independently of the fact that no argument can be pushed to an extreme, I apprehend experience will show that, once admitted, the effect of force of character and perseverance will be generally equal to overcoming the previous disadvantages. Perhaps in the long run the ease with which more educated boys would master the early part of the course, would tend to slacken their own energies and put them yet more on an equality with their less favored rivals.

A second and stronger reason for a low standard is greater facility of moulding. Remember that we have here before us no mere question of a general education, or carrying on to perfection, in a higher institution, the work already well begun in a lower. The Naval educator has, in any event, to begin at the beginning and fashion, for a special and singular purpose, crude material into a highly tempered weapon fitted for a life and actions which, in their ideal, call for the highest qualities of vigor, endurance and intelligence; (I don't say knowledge). Under such circumstances it is an advantage that the character and mind should have received as little previous bent as may be.

For these reasons I should prefer that the requirements for admission should be confined to such knowledge as is not easily acquired after childhood, or, if so acquired, requires a very disproportionate time. Reading; writing a good hand; spelling; facility in the operations of arithmetic up to and through decimal fractions; such will indicate, if not the whole, at least the level of attainment that I would require of the candidate. For the same reason, i.e. facility of moulding and shaping character, a matter quite as important as mere brain development in the question before us, I would distinctly prefer lowering the maximum age of admission, (now 18 years).

The lad coming thus into the hands of his trainers, it is necessary, as I have said, before considering the course of education, to consider what sort of man you wish him to be when he enters the service; and what possibilities of future development he should be prepared for. This involves the question of what the ideal naval officer of the present day should be; a question that must be dealt with here, to bring out clearly my idea.

I am persuaded that in our theory of education we have failed in this country to recognize that the progress of the mechanical sciences, and the vast change thereby made in naval vessels and their armaments, as well as in other means of warfare, have made necessary the organization of corps of specialists. Recognizing and dazzled by the stupendous nature of the changes made, and the wonderful things accomplished by the labors of science, those who have had the direction of our naval education, or who have exerted influence upon that direction, seem to run away with the idea that every naval officer, having to use these engines of offense or defense which the student or mechanic has put in his hands, should therefore be able to follow out the long train of laborious thought, be familiar with all the practical processes, by which each of these mighty engines has been conceived and produced. Singularly enough, in the only case in which an education distinctly special has been laid down, that for the present Engineer Corps, the same confusion in adapting means to ends prevails; and the country is now laboriously educating to a very considerable point of attainment a number of men whose duties for many years, and till middle life, cannot rise beyond those discharged competently, all over the land, by men wholly uneducated, in the usual sense.

It is necessary, then, to look forward to the end, and consider really what you should require a sea officer of the Navy to be. We have actually gotten in the Navy, by constantly adding here a little, there a little, to a pass in which we think that each military sea officer, or to use the technical term, each line officer, should present in his own person a compendium of mathematics including its highest branches, its applications to numerous recondite physical problems, considerable knowledge of the physical and mechanical sciences, and an intimate acquaintance with the arts of the manufacturer; all in addition to a command of his own profession proper. Failing this, so many say, he must descend from the high position occupied by him and his predecessors for these centuries past and become the simple drudge of others whose minds have received a more rigorous and deeper, though often narrower, culture. Nor is this a mere thought; only the mental impossibility of cramming more study into a four years' course prevents an attempt to carry the theory into effect.

Let me then try to state clearly what qualities, in my opinion, you should especially wish in the line officer of the Navy. I scarcely think I can err in assigning to the foremost place moral power; strength to control self and others; fearlessness in responsibility and in danger; self reliance; promptitude in action; readiness of resource; calmness amid excitement. No amount of mental caliber, far less any mere knowledge, can compensate for a deficiency in moral force in our profession. I wish carefully to guard myself from implying that knowledge does not increase many of these powers, as it increases for example the resources, or enables accurately to measure danger. My point is this: will those habits of the student, the constant, strenuous application, the amount of confinement and closet work involved, tend to make a man more fit or less fit for the storm or the battle? I believe they tend to impede the growth of the class of moral powers needed at sea; to promote caution unduly; to substitute calculation for judgment; to create trust in formulas rather than in one's self. In truth the matter may be shortly stated thus, that a man does best that which he constantly does; moves more easily and better in scenes to which he is accustomed; and that it is given to few men to be equally at home on the deck and in the closet, in action and in meditation. Yet this is what our Navy seems to aim at.

Next to moral power follows, in my opinion, physical vigor. Few probably will dispute the necessity of the latter, or the effect which it exercises upon the faculties of the soul. It is most impressive to read of the triumph of spirit over matter, as in the case of the typical naval hero Nelson; yet even Nelson had to yield in the body, though his will remained unconquered and good; though lesser men would have been brought down long before. Although however I fancy I see injury that has been done to bodily health by over study among officers, I do not think it is as dangerous to the physique as to the morale.

I come last to what very many put first, i.e. the intellectual equipment; the acquired knowledge, I mean, as well as the natural ability. I must here save myself from being misunderstood, by saying that I put knowledge last, not because I undervalue that, or would accept less than a very respectable amount of a kind I will mention later, but simply in comparison with bodily and moral power in a naval officer. No one would be supposed to undervalue physical courage because he said a clear head and legal knowledge were of more value to a consulting lawyer.

The knowledge that is necessary to a naval line officer is simply and solely that which enables him to discharge his many duties intelligently and thoroughly. Any information that goes beyond this point is after all simply culture, which, however desirable in itself, must not be confounded with essentials. This is true although the special culture may be of a kind very closely akin to his profession. For instance the manufacture of ordnance, the intricate questions connected with explosives, have a very close connection with the military part of his business. Yet to say that an exhaustive and exact knowledge of the various processes by which the finished gun and the proved powder are furnished to his hand and of the rapid though gradual advance made in each, is necessary, is to occupy ground that is not tenable. Similarly on the sailor side of the profession, it may certainly be said that an accomplished seaman should understand enough of the principles which govern naval architecture and determine the qualities of a vessel, to guide him to some conclusions, above the level of a guess, as to the causes of unsatisfactory behavior in any circumstances; but it is going a long way further to claim that he must be prepared to enter into an elaborate explanation of the method by which those principles are derived and formulated. Yet the statement that the two branches of scientific research and effort named above are, and must continue to be, the work of two classes of specialists, to me a most simple and evident fact, is practically not recognized as yet by our naval educators.

I confess to a feeling of mingled impatience and bitterness when I hear the noble duties and requirements of a naval officer's career ignored, and an attempt made to substitute for them the wholly different aims and faculties of the servant of science. The comparatively small scale on which those duties are now performed, the fancied impossibility of a great war, the pitiful condition of efficiency into which the material of the navy has been allowed to fall, have all helped to blind our eyes to the magnificence of the war seaman's career. At the same time science has been, and still is, achieving her magnificent conquests; and men, as always, in the presence of the achievements of the moment forget the triumphs of the past. No wonder the line officers of the navy are themselves carried away by an amazed humility which falsely dwarfs their own profession. Yet history does not countenance the idea that an untroubled assurance of peace is a guarantee that war will not come; in the little things of the naval profession of our day and country may be even now the preparation for events as great as those in which a naval captain changed the career of Napoleon. Let us then, in estimating the ideal for which we are to train the raw lad placed in our hands, turn our eyes from the things we too often know to be, the wretched character of most of our ships, the aversion to sea duty, the amount of time passed slothfully in port. Let us forget for a moment the mortification and lack of interest which follows from these, and which are common to all military service in time of peace, and let us look at those duties which are involved in keeping the sea in time of war. For those duties our youth must be trained, and any study that tends to unfit for them should be discontinued.

The officers who, whether in command or in subordinate military position, are to handle and fight a modern ship of war, must have a thorough acquaintance with the general construction of vessels, and with the peculiarities, if there be any of the particular ship. Equally they should all know how to handle familiarly the apparatus for controlling and directing her movements, including in these both sails and engines, the latter a point heretofore sadly neglected. It will be their business to find out speedily how the ship will act under various circumstances of wind, weather, trim, speed, &c., so that they may be able to know what they can expect her to do in any case; indeed it would be well if that familiarity with her movements became so great as to dispense ordinarily with conscious thought or calculation. A similar close knowledge of the armament and all other equipments is necessary.

For this portion of the requisite knowledge, how great an amount of scientific power is required? Naval construction is involved, naval architecture scarcely at all. Some acquaintance with the mechanical powers and the modes of their applications, but scarcely enough to dignify by the name of science. That the knowledge sufficient to run and care for marine steam engines can be acquired by men of very little education is a matter of daily experience; although the naval system of our country has continued to surround a simple enough practical matter, very different from the designing and building of machinery, with a glamour of science and difficulty which does not exist. Some knowledge of electricity will be needed, if the torpedo form a part of the ship's offensive equipment. In all this my contention is not only that science, beyond some simple elementary knowledge of principles which can be applied practically with the resources of the ship, is unnecessary, but also that the attempt to carry it farther involves the loss of time that had better be applied to practical uses; further that the habit of the student in the laboratory, or over formulas, is as a rule an injury to qualities and habits of mind more necessary to a seaman and a military man.

There is, however, one branch of knowledge, intimately connected with the duties of the sea officer, to which I hesitate to apply a limit of strict necessity. I mean the subjects generally embraced by us under the head of Navigation, with its handmaid Surveying. The importance to an officer of familiarity with all the means by which a ship's position may be determined, and course laid with accuracy, such knowledge as in intricate navigation will insure the most perfect adjustment of carefulness and boldness, is apparent at a glance. The problems relating to the deviations of the compass, especially if ironclads and iron ships are to continue in the navy, make it desirable that the various causes which lead to or modify these errors should be thoroughly understood in theory, and not merely by rule of thumb. The knowledge should be such as to keep an officer wide awake to any chance of new errors creeping in unawares. Again scientific surveying, it seems to me, falls naturally into the province of the officer whose career is to belong primarily to the sea and to the ship, and not to those classes of specialists with whom, as I shall afterwards indicate, the seafaring part of the naval career is to be of secondary importance. If our Government should ever determine, as it is to be hoped it will, to use its navy in times of peace for the making much needed surveys in distant parts of the world, it is evidently much to be desired that the officers who will have to go in charge of the ships should be fully qualified to do all the work of the survey proper. At this particular place I may say that so much knowledge of botany, mineralogy and kindred topics as would enable a reconnaissance of the natural capabilities of remote countries to accompany the report of a survey, would increase the power of usefulness in a line officer. I do not advocate making them compulsory, but would make provision for imparting, and offer inducements for acquiring, such knowledge after graduation. This agrees fully with the principle which I hope to show underlies my whole argument, viz.: that in the corps of line officers, whose business is to handle, navigate, discipline and fight the ships, should be found all the acquirements necessary to discharge the other duties, save only the surgeon's; or if the statement in those terms seem objectionable, let us say that the other corps should so far acquire the specialties of the line as to be able to bear their share in performing the duties.

I have so far written, not thoroughly nor in detail, but in a general manner and sufficiently for the purpose of such an essay as this, upon the three great heads of Seamanship, Gunnery and Navigation under which the qualifications of a naval officer fall: being careful to say distinctly that under the first head I include such a practical knowledge of the steam engine as will enable him to take charge of the engines of the ship, and render unnecessary the maintenance of a special corps of engineer officers for that exceedingly simple office. There is worthier work for a suitable corps of naval engineers.

And having thus discussed them, I again turn and ask; why this mighty cry for science, in the modern limited sense of the term; limited yet further in our use to the mechanical and physical sciences, as an indispensable part of the mental equipment of a war seaman? Granted, as every one must grant, that such science has its necessary place somewhere in naval administration, what is there in it that the seaman cannot handle and fight his ship, I don't merely say without it, but just as well without it as with it. Yet handling and fighting his ship is his business; and if so, in his education no time should be given to any pursuit which does not lead

directly up to those two things, if such pursuit be at the expense of occupations which do lead up to them. Yet just this, under the delusive cry of
science, we are more and more doing.

There are yet three other heads under which the mental acquirements of a naval officer fall: the English studies, Naval Tactics and Foreign Languages. Although none of these are dignified by the name of
science, few will find fault with the extent to which they are now carried at Annapolis. About Naval Tactics I shall here say nothing. If I be
asked, in my own words, how the English studies or the acquirements of
Foreign Languages help a man to handle and fight his ship, I will reply
that a taste for these two pursuits tends to give breadth of thought and
loftiness of spirit; the English directly, the Foreign Languages by opening
their literature. The ennobling effect of such pursuits upon the sentiment
and intellect of the seaman helps, I think, to develop a generous pride,
a devotion to lofty ideals, which cannot fail to have a beneficial effect
upon a profession which possesses, and in its past history has illustrated
in a high degree, many of the elements of heroism and grandeur. The
necessarily materialistic character of mechanical science tends rather to
narrowness and low ideals.

I here mention International and Prize Law as necessary to the mental furniture of a line officer, but only lest I may be thought to intention-
ally omit them. I do not care to urge their importance, as none will be
found to question it.

Do I then undervalue science? Do I ignore the great changes it has
made in the appliances and system of naval warfare, or deny the necessity
to the service of men thoroughly imbued with its spirit and acquainted
with its truths? Not at all, I simply say that while the processes, by which
the results of scientific research are obtained, are laborious and difficult,
the results themselves, for naval purposes, are instruments easy of comprehension and intelligent use; while the practical use of them, under
the varied and often exciting conditions of sea and battle service, calls
for other and very different qualities and experience than those of the

student or the mechanic. Consequently devotion to science and the production of the instruments of warfare, from the ship itself downwards, should be the portion of certain, relatively small, classes of specialists.

Here I must revert again to my assertion of the pre-eminent importance to the sea officer of that which for want of a better word, I call moral force. When his ship is equipped and his knowledge of her powers complete, the most important part of the line officer's work is yet before him. I might almost say all his real work is before him; that which has been done is only preparation.

The organizing and disciplining of the crew, the management under all circumstances of the great machine which a ship is, call for a very high order of character, whether natural or acquired; capacity for governing men, for dealing with conflicting tempers and interests jarring in a most artificial mode of life; self possession and habit of command in danger, in sudden emergencies, in the tumult and probable horrors of a modern naval action; sound judgment which can take risks calmly, yet risk no more than is absolutely necessary; sagacity to divine the probable movements of an enemy, to provide against future wants, to avoid or compel action as may be wished; moral courage, to be shown in fearlessness of responsibility, in readiness to either act or not act, regardless of censure whether from above or below; quickness of eye and mind, the intuitive perception of danger or advantage, the ready instinct which seizes the proper means in either case: all these are faculties not born in every man, not perfected in any man save by the long training of habit— a fact to which the early history of all naval wars bears witness. Now this training can only be acquired by an active pursuit of the profession, and not in the closet; while on the other hand the achievements of the student and the man of science cannot as a rule be wrought in the cabin of the seaman. The studious and scientific intellect is not that which most readily attaches itself to a naval life, or if forced into it attains eminence therein; and the attempt to combine the two has upon the whole been a failure, except where it has succeeded in reducing both to mediocrity in the individual.

The record of the Naval Academy may be pretty confidently searched to prove that distinguished academical standing conveys no necessary promise of professional excellence; while on the other hand very admirable naval aptitude is shown in many cases by men, intelligent indeed, but not students. The fact is obscured somewhat by the worthlessness, in a professional point of view, of the tail end of many classes; which however only proves the common experience that there are many irremediable blockheads in the world, as well as many men who are fit for no profession, utterly idle and good for nothing. On the other hand a conscientious student and able man can attain respectability in almost any line. I apprehend, however, that the memory of most who know the service will supply enough instances in either direction to substantiate the main statement; and the annals of the service at large bear the same record of men of patient research, scientific habit of mind and constant study, who have as such rendered invaluable benefit to the navy, but who yet did not command its confidence as sea officers.

Moreover, when the care of instructors and the conscientious pains of the student have turned out a man well equipped to begin a scientific career, with distinct reference to the navy, what use is made of him? After the maiden cruise, which, if not too long, would be a positive benefit as a relaxation from study, and means of acquiring sympathy with naval habits of thought, and knowledge of naval necessities, the young man, presumed to have a turn for study and science, begins a career of alternate sea service and shore duty which renders connected application to any one pursuit impossible. Take, for instance, one who would make ordnance and its kindred subjects a specialty. For three years he may be in circumstances which enable him to see and learn, and he advances rapidly; then he is caught up and sent to sea, out of the way of every thing. He has neither access to the periodical or other literature which he cannot afford for himself, nor opportunity to see and keep up his acquaintance with the practical processes chronicled by those periodicals. The atmosphere around him virtually precludes study; for while we may deny that it is impossible to study aboard ship, on the general ground that where there's a will there's a way, it is none the less true that few actively pursue study, as distinct from reading, under the conditions of ship and mess life. The temptations to pleasure, the novelty of many scenes, the constant distractions, the close and heavy air of the sleeping apartments, all tend to compel men to social out door life, and to deter from strong mental effort.

I have wished, so far, to make the point that not only does the habit of life of the student unfit for the life of the deck, but also that the life of the ship interferes vitally with the habits of the student. The result is sometimes seen in the eagerness with which students escape, or enter other branches of the profession, when they can. I would provide, at least partially, a place for such in the navy.

There is yet another reason which I think strengthens my argument in favor of corps of specialists. There are physical causes which unfit men for the active life of the sea officer, but which leave their minds as clear as ever. Physical infirmities, the inroads of age, do undoubtedly often impair the efficiency of the seamen, and of the nerve force, while leaving the intellect untouched. This truth is recognized by the retiring schemes of most great military services, which compel officers to leave the active line of the profession at a fixed age—as well as for cause at any age. Recognize clearly, however, certain classes of men in the service, whose particular capacity lies in brain work or aptitude for the mechanical science, and those men will not need to be retired for causes which do not affect their efficiency; though they may that of the seaman.

Assuming the principle of specialties is granted, I come next to consider how many classes of such specialists I would have in the service.

Premising that all graduates of the Academy should be line officers, there would, under that general head, be three such specialties: Construction, Engineering, and Ordnance officers. I do not feel sure but incline to believe that Construction and Engineering would ultimately come under one head on the Navy Register; the Senior officer of the Corps knowing and using properly the particular capacities of each officer. I shall hereafter in this paper consider the two classes as one, under the name of Engineer officers.

In addition to the above there would be yet another class of officers, requiring different, but less highly intellectual qualities, who would form the Pay Corps of the navy. It has never seemed to me reasonable to assign line officers indiscriminately, and for a cruise only, to duty as pay-masters; but on the other hand I have never seen any reason to doubt that one man could perform the duties both of watch officer and pay-master, particularly if spared divisional work. Hence I would select from the graduates of each year such man or men to be assigned to the Pay Corps as the wants of that body may demand; he, like the others, to retain his position and lineal rank as a line officer, to do duty and have all the consideration and responsibility of a line officer, while at the same time assuming charge of the pay department in his particular ship.

The officers of the Engineer and Ordnance Corps would also retain their position and rank as established by graduation; but it would be understood that sea service was to be with them the exception and not the rule, and that the main occupation of their life should be the study, development, and oversight of the material of the service. After the first cruise, a term of one year of sea service to every five of shore duty would, in my judgment, be sufficient, up to the grade of Lieut.-Com-mander, after which no rule need be laid down. The amount of sea ser-vice indicated would tend to keep them from losing sight of the practical exigencies of a ship, a fault which has often been found with the present naval constructors. Whenever so ordered to sea they should take the rank and duties to which their lineal rank assigns them, but sea service should cease when the grade of Commander is reached.

The officers of the Pay Corps, on the contrary, should go to sea exactly as the line officers who belong to no special corps, up to the age at which he would, by seniority, be executive officer of any ship to which he would be ordered. The two duties of executive and paymaster would be too onerous when joined; so at this period of his career I would give the pay officer the choice of remaining in the pay corps with the advantage of less sea service, or of casting in his lot with the sea corps, with the advantage of command. During the remainder of this paper I shall speak of those now called line officers and of the pay corps under the one title of the "Sea Corps."

In these details I will seem to depart from my subject; independently however, of the fact that the word education must not be too closely restricted to direct teaching by others, but rather extended to all influences by which the desired results or qualities are educed, I feel myself under the necessity of defending the system I propose by pointing out briefly the ultimate results at which that system aims. As far as I know there is a good deal of novelty in the general scheme, and novelty's charms are, in naval eyes, doubtful.

My aim, then, is this: To recognize and provide for the existing and perfecting of a small body of specialists, but at the same time to provide that every commissioned officer attached to a ship, save the surgeons, should be capable, some more, some less, but each capable of every military and sea duty suitable to his lineal rank. That they should all be charged with the execution of the same, and should all be in one line of rank; the distinction of corps being internal to that line.

Promotion would go on in that line and not by corps.

Having thus developed my aim and the reasonings which have led me to it, I now proceed to consider the course through which I would carry the successful candidate for admission to a naval career; I may as well say the candidate for admission to the Naval Academy, as I base the training I advocate upon that pursued there.

The number of cadet midshipmen now allowed in the service is determined by the number of Congressional districts; one being allowed to each district, and the appointment vesting in its Representative. I have no change to advocate here. The majority will probably owe their appointment to political or personal interest; but however objectionable this motive, we are not likely to find many members of Congress with the inclination or time to determine the Appointment by other reasons than favor. As there have been some, however, who have shown a desire to select the most worthy applicant, I should like to see the navy department, when notifying a representative that a vacancy exists in his district, add some advice to this general effect: That in the opinion of the Navy Department a simple educational test was of no great value in discriminating between applicants; and that good health, wholeness and vigor of body, and, where they could be ascertained, in dictations of pluck, perseverance, taking the lead in a manly, not a vicious way, among equals in age, were of more worth than intellectual forwardness, as showing the stuff of which a good officer could be made.

Probably the most rigorous sifting by the course I shall propose would yet graduate fully as many as would be needed to fill the yearly vacancies in all the different corps; and it must not be forgotten that a certain number of appointments, technically styled "at large" are allowed to the President. As the system I propose will only permit a limited number to be graduated, it might be just, or at least kind, to faithful officers of the government to increase the number of the Presidential appointees, so as to allow the sons of such officers to compete for the prize of graduation and a commission. Opposed as I am to a high standard of admission, and proposing, as I have above, that every graduate shall possess adequate knowledge to superintend the running, care, and all ordinary repairs of a steam engine, I would of course do away with the cadet engineers of the present system, who are appointed by a competitive examination before the Academic Board. The corps of Engineer Officers which I propose would necessarily possess the power of running an engine, but their proper duties would be of the far higher order which embraces the designing and construction of ships and engines. The Navy needs a first rate, but comparatively very small, body of such men.

The appointees from the districts, who shall pass the required physical and educational tests, would all form one body under the title of "cadets," "naval cadets," or "midshipmen," whichever may be preferred, I shall throughout speak of them as midshipmen. The existing course, being based upon the plan of having cadet midshipmen and cadet engineers from the start, will need considerable mordification.

At first the officers and professors will be wholly ignorant of the capacities of the youths. The first years' course therefore must be the same for all, and yet so designed as to oppose no hindrance to following up immediately either course, as soon as the specialties have been determined.

For the first year, then, I propose the following studies:

> 1 Mathematics,
> 2 English,
> 3 Mechanical Drawing.

This omits the Modern Languages from the present first year's course. I think I shall have the support of the instructors in French in deprecating, as waste of time, teaching that language before the mixed multitude that forms an ordinary fourth class has been sifted. The time gained from the languages should be devoted to Mathematics and English, more particularly to the former, with a view to completing the course earlier in the second, (or third class,) year than is now the case.

By the middle of the first year it will be clearly seen in most cases how men will stand. The class should then be divided into two sections, and the higher section should not be kept back by the less able men, many of whom, under this system, will not enter the service at all.

The duties of the officers charged with the drills and discipline will, as it does now, lead them to note the bearing and capacities of each man. I would not have these taken into account in the first year, but in the second I shall most distinctly advocate this, as yet unknown, feature in the tests.

Mechanical is preferred to free hand drawing, as the knowledge of it will be essential to those selected for the Engineer and Ordnance Corps.

At the end of the year midshipmen who fail to attain a certain standard of merit will be dropped from the Academy, or else turned back into the succeeding class, according to the decision of the Academic Board in the special case.

For the second year the course would embrace the following branches, for all midshipmen.

> Mathematics,
> English,
> Modern Languages,
> Drawing,
> Steam,
> Mechanics.

This omits from the present course Physics and Chemistry as taught in that year. The time thereby gained I would allot first to Drawing, second to Modern Languages, third to Steam.

It is my hope and belief that, without materially diminishing the present Mathematical course, the time gained in the first (fourth class) year, and the superior ability of the upper sections, would permit of finishing the course in time to take up and complete a very simple course of Mechanics. This last should not extend beyond that necessary for an intelligent charge of a sea officer's duty, and will not necessitate a knowledge of mathematics beyond algebra, geometry and trigonometry. If, however, this cannot be done, then Steam must yield to Mechanics and wait for the third year.

Additional time is here allotted to Modern Languages beyond that now given; this will partially compensate the loss in the first year, and being devoted to the better part of the now reduced class, will perhaps in the end go as far as that at present assigned. The same remark applies to Drawing, which gains considerably; being carried through the second half of the year.

In this year the drill and executive officers should note and mark the midshipmen, as to bearing and attention to duty. The effect on class standing should as yet be small, for it will not be possible to give to the third class the same scrutiny of individuals as to the upper classes. Marked excellency or defect can however be noted; and a concurrent unfavorable opinion on the part of the drill officers should ensure failure to pass on to the higher classes. Let us not forget that the aim is to make officers, and let us no more see the practical absurdity of a worthless man's passing into the service, merely because he can stand an examination in books. No observer of the Academy is unaware that men of high class standing are too frequently indifferent to their conduct as officers.

At the end of the two years I would put into operation a plan suggested by a distinguished Superintendent of the Academy, which is as follows. The probable number of annual vacancies in the grade of Ensign, for all Corps, due to deaths, retirements, or other causes, should be estimated by some expert in such calculations, and only that number should be allowed to continue the course with a view to entering the navy. Such number would as a rule be the head men of the class, and that class standing would be determined almost entirely by mental proficiency. I would put upon it a check to which I have alluded above, namely, that if the preponderating opinion of the whole body of executive and drill officers should be adverse to any man's fitness for the service, that opinion should exclude him, and the next man in class standing should have the vacancy. It will be observed that this check is very different from a power given to the executive officers to choose out men, who fail to attain adequate class standing, to take the place of such as have that standing but who, in the opinion of the officers, have less aptitude for the service. I do not think, that in the first two years and among the large number of midshipmen in the lower classes, officers can distinguish with nice precision relative aptitude; the time given to drills and other duties is very small compared to that given to studies, and the check I advocate would be rarely exercised and then in pronounced instances. It would deal also mainly with those cases of general inaptitude, so easy to recognize, so hard to define, and not with special offences, which are sufficiently provided for by the general discipline of the school supervised by the Navy Department.

The word "sad" is scarcely too strong when applied to the sight of the number of youths yearly turned into the service from the Naval Academy so greatly in excess of the demand. Granting, (which cannot be granted), that no large portion of them are undesirable additions to the Navy, it is sad to think of the hopeless future before them; sad to think of merit weighed down by a mass of demerit above; sad to think of the country depending upon a profession which demands above all buoyant energy and hope, but whose prizes under the present system cannot be reached, till all the buoyancy, energy and hope have been sickened out by weary waiting. Some relation between demand and supply would be established by the system advocated; and the country, whose interest in the Navy is commensurate with its interest in the capacity of its officers, should see such a relation fixed.

With the entrance of this chosen body of midshipmen upon their third year the separation between the sea and the other Corps must be made, and the difficulty of determining the course of instruction is greatly increased. The separate courses now laid down for cadet midshipmen and cadet engineers must be combined, and as I do not propose to lengthen the Academic term of four years, the difficulty of this combination is apparent. There are, however, certain considerations which tend to diminish this trouble. The mass of the class, intended for sea service principally, will not need Calculus, nor Mechanics beyond the elementary course of the first two years. The time thus gained, which will be seen by a reference to the present course to be considerable, (10 hours a week) can be given to Steam, English and Modern Languages. I speak of these in their order of importance from my point of view. The greater portion, say six hours, should be given to Steam, of which the sea officer is to have a thorough practical knowledge. Two hours additional to the present allowance, will be given to both English and Modern Languages; with the proviso that if further instruction is considered necessary in Drawing, and I think it likely then Modern languages must give up this additional period to Drawing for one or both terms of the year.

So much for the Sea Corps. For the midshipmen intended for the Corps of Engineering and Ordnance the difficulty is greater, but I think not insuperable. Mechanics for them cannot be disregarded; but it is to be remembered that while they are to have such a knowledge of seamanship as to be safe deck officers, yet the sea is not to be their chief aim, nor will they command at sea. Time therefore can be gained from book seamanship, both in this year and the next. The same remark, I think, applies to Astronomy, a subject which will have little place in their future pursuits. The sea officer, who is to be navigator and surveyor, needs, as a good foundation, knowledge of the motions of the heavenly bodies; not so one whose life is to be mainly spent on shore in pursuit of science of a different kind. From Astronomy and Seamanship, then, I think to gain the time for Steam which the Sea Corps gains from Mechanics.

Additional time for English and for Modern Languages, gained by the Sea Corps, would not be so much needed by the Engineer and Ordnance Corps, for two reasons: First, the time for English is assigned to make up for that which I have to take from the first class course of the Sea Corps, but do not propose to take from the other corps in that year. Second, it is to be remembered that the most intellectual men of the class will have been chosen for these corps; and it is probable that in the knowledge of French, save accent, they will be well abreast the rest of their class, under an arrangement of sections according to proficiency.

This same greater capacity leads me to think that the loss of Physics and Chemistry, dropped from the third class year, can be very largely made up to the midshipmen chosen for the Engineer and Ordnance Corps. It must be remembered that you have, in place of a large class of unequal capacity, a very few picked men, probably not over four or five, not tied down to a low average rate of advance, and to whom the teacher can give a degree of personal attention now unattainable. For the Sea Corps I would make no attempt to take up Physics and Chemistry, but would leave the subjects to be pursued in connection with a post-graduate course, after the first cruise, in the manufacture and handling of torpedoes.

Before tabulating the course for the second class year, it is desirable to say a word upon the study of Modern Languages, which ends with this year. The French language is of importance not only colloquially, but also as giving the key to a large scientific literature. As such it is useful to both the sea and the more scientific Corps. With Spanish the case is different. A knowledge of it is useful, because it is the language of many maritime countries, and particularly of several republics, large and small, in whose welfare it is the policy of our government to manifest a friendly interest; but scientifically it is of small value. I have therefore dropped Modern Languages from the second term of this year for the Scientific Corps, retaining it for the Sea Corps. I do not however specify which language is to be pursued. It is well known that many youths do not now attain a good knowledge of French; such should continue French, and only those sufficiently advanced should take up Spanish at all. Of course they would be allowed extra credit for the course.

For the third (or second class) year then the course proposal would be as follows:

First Term.

Engineering and Ordnance Corps
Seamanship . . . 1 period (The period is two hours; there are
      fifteen periods in one week; three in one day.)
Ordnance and Gunnery . . . 1 period
Astronomy . . . 1 period
Mechanics (Calculus) . . . 5 periods
Steam . . . 3 periods
English Studies . . . 1 period per month
Modern Languages . . . 4 periods

Sea Corps
Seamanship . . . 2 periods

Ordnance and Gunnery . . . 1 period
Astronomy . . . 3 periods
Steam . . . 3 periods
English Studies . . . 1&1 period per month
Modern Languages . . . 4 periods leaving 1 period to be given to
    Mod. Languages or Drawing as may seem best.

SECOND TERM.

Engineering and Ordnance Corps
Seamanship . . . 1 period
Naval Tactics . . . 1 period
Ordnance . . . 1 period
Steam . . . 4 periods
Mechanics . . . 5 periods
Physics . . . 3 periods
English . . . 1 period per month

Sea Corps
Seamanship . . . 3 periods
Naval Tactics . . . 1 period
Ordnance . . . 1 period
Steam . . . 4 periods
English Studies . . . 1&1 period per month
Modern Languages . . . 3 periods per month
Drawing . . . 2 periods

It is probable that to give proper instructions in Seamanship and Astronomy to the Engineer and Ordnance Corps, with the limited time allowed
by this program, a very carefully considered compendium, in the shape
of a new text book, would have to be drawn up for each subject. I think
there is no impossibility in the way of doing this.

With the beginning of the final year I should adopt a new system with the Sea Corps. The theoretical instruction in Seamanship and Steam should now be followed up by constant practical exercises, through the ships that should be attached to the school. In order to this I would give up the third period, or afternoon of each day to such practical work; to which should be added the drill time, in all three or four hours a day.

To gain this afternoon time, in all ten hours, or "five periods," to use the terminology of the school, I would give up the subjects of Heat and Light in the Department of Physics, Spanish in Modern Languages, and one period each from Seamanship and Steam.

To defend a step which will probably provoke much adverse comment I must say, what we all know to be the case, that no dependence can be placed upon cruising after graduation to supply this necessary practice. The exigencies of the service, the fancies or indifference of individual admirals or captains, keep ships often idle for long periods in ports. Some captains interest themselves in seeing that their young officers acquire practical experience in their profession; others do not. No certain reliance can be placed upon opportunities after graduation.

To obtain these I would unhesitatingly make the sacrifice of study hours and of the branches named for the Sea Corps.

As the lower classes would not take part in these exercises, the necessary force must come from the general service; and nowhere, I believe, would a hundred good seamen and twenty-five or thirty firemen be more fruitfully bestowed than for such purpose at the Naval school.

Nor, though the drill time is to be used for these exercises, does it follow that the first class are to have none of the usual drills. Let us imagine a class of twenty-five destined for the Sea Corps, and a favorable day for exercises of every kind.

1 drills a company of infantry.
2 " batteries of light artillery.
1 " a squadron of boats.

10 go to steamer to run engines.

4   "   " to be maneuvered under steam and sail, to take deck
    and forecastle alternately.

6 to go to sailing sloop where they will take deck or forecastle.

It is not necessary to elaborate, though one is tempted to do so; the combinations of drills that can be made will be innumerable. Those that are to take charge of the three drills first named, in which midshipmen of the lower classes are to be engaged after 4 P.M., need not lose the previous time. They can join any of the latter three exercises and be sent ashore by one of the Academy steam launches, after taking their share, in time for the ordinary drills. Nor is a young mind distressed by thus going from one occupation to another, as older ones sometimes are.

Two things are evident:

1st. Every first classman will thus have abundant opportunity of bearing a principal part many times in every kind of drill and practical exercise.

PRESENT SYSTEM.	PROPOSED SYSTEM.
1 Captain,	1 Captain (Sea Corps)
1 Executive,	1 Executive (Sea, Eng. or Ord.)
1 Navigator,	1 Navigator (Sea Corps).
4 Watch (and Division) officers,	2 Watch & Div. (Sea, Eng. or Ord.)
1 Paymaster,	1 Watch and Paymaster (Sea Corps)
1 Engineer,	1 Watch & Eng. (Sea, Eng. or Ord.)
9	7

2nd. The duties of subordinate officers, lieutenants of companies, in charge of single boats, &c., will be devolved on second classmen, who now rarely fill any more important function than high private.

The practical exercises of Saturday will remain for the advantage of the Engineer and Ordnance Midshipmen; it will be remembered that the special practical work of these, viz., the designing, construction and care of material, must come after graduation.

To gain the required time for exercises in the second term, I would omit English studies (Public Law) from the present program having already provided for it in the second class course.

For the Engineer and Ordnance Corps I would leave the course very nearly as it now stands in the Academy program. Spanish, for reasons already given, would disappear, and the time be assigned to Gunnery and Ordnance.

The very great amount of time now given to Steam should be distributed, according to the Corps to which the midshipman is destined, to Naval Architecture, designing and construction of machinery, or the more advanced study of ordnance problems. For, as these two classes of midshipmen have been before together separated from the mass of the students, the time has come with the closing year to divide them one from the other.

The tabulated result would be the following weekly program of studies for the First Class of Midshipmen.

FIRST TERM.

Sea Corps
Naval Construction . . . 2 periods
Ordnance . . . 2 periods
Steam . . . 2 periods
Navigation . . . 4 periods

Engineer and Ordnance
Naval Construction . . . 3 periods
Ordnance, Naval Architecture, and Steam . . . 7 periods
Physics . . . 2 periods
Mechanics . . . 3 periods

SECOND TERM.

<u>Sea Corps</u>
Seamanship . . . 2 periods
Ordnance . . . 2 periods
Steam . . . 2 periods
Navigation and Survey . . . 4 periods

<u>Engineer and Ordnance</u>
Seamanship . . . 1 period
Naval Architecture, Ordnance, or Steam . . . 6 periods
Physics . . . 1 period
Mechanics . . . 1 period
English (Public) law . . . 2 periods
Navigation . . . 2 periods

During the last two years the conduct of Midshipmen at drills, exercises, and daily duty should be carefully scrutinized by the executive and drill officers. The opinion of each officer for each month should be expressed in a mark, and the combined marks of the different officers should establish a final annual figure, representing the aptitude of the midshipmen in determining class standing. I consider it a very grave defect in the present system that the fact of a midshipman's displaying in a marker degree the qualities of a "good officer," attention, alertness and force, has no effect upon his standing. On the contrary, inertness, indifference, or failure to control those under him, do not in the least damage him.

I have thus traced the course, both of studies and practical exercises, which would constitute the education of a midshipman up to the time of his graduation from the Academy. It is not desirable, in an essay of this kind, to go largely into details, nor to defend such details as may have been laid down; nor is it to be expected that any one man will be likely to deal satisfactorily with so complicated a subject as the details. I therefore here leave the Academic course with the following resume of my general plan.

1. A low standard of acquirement for admission.
2. All admitted to form one Corps of Midshipmen.
3. The course for the first two years to be as far as possible simplified and to be common to all.
4. At the end of two years, retention only of so many as are yearly required to fill vacancies in the grade of Ensign, and the separation of those who remain into three Corps; Engineers, Ordnance and Sea Corps. The education of each corps to be as thorough as possible in its own special-ties; Seamanship, Practical Gunnery, Navigation, Astron-omy and Surveying being the specialties of the Sea Corps; Ordnance in all its branches of the Ordnance; Naval Architecture and Marine Steam Engine building of the Engineer Corps. At the same time each corps is to receive such instruction in the specialties of the others as may be necessary and possible.
5. The last year of the Sea Corps to be wholly given to profes-sional and largely to practical work.
6. Aptitude for service and officer-like bearing to have an effect upon class standing, i.e., upon future rank.
7. The Pay Corps to come from the Sea Corps.

After graduation the midshipmen should have the usual leave, and then be ordered to sea-going ships for one or two years' sea service; during this period to be called midshipmen. I would have the Navy Department direct that during this first cruise, the commanding officer should assign each to duty as watch, navigation and engineer officers in turn, and for such periods as may be deemed best; and on leaving the ship should, in the usual letter, state what opportunities have thus been given him to continue the education begun at the school.

At the expiration of the cruise, the examination now customary to be held before a mixed board, taken from the Service at large and the Board of the Academy. I do not approve of the present system, by which these examinations are held by the Academic Board alone. The result of this examination, combined with the class standing at graduation, should finally determine lineal rank; unless in one contingency yet to be mentioned. A failure to pass should, as now, cause the midshipman to be dropped to the following class.

A serious difficulty will before this be seen by the reader of this paper. How is class standing in one class to be determined among men whose studies are different?

There is but one answer. When the studies are common to each, though pursued in different degrees, as Seamanship and Steam, the common value will obtain in each case. When the studies are peculiar to one Corps, give them value as an elective course, or perhaps more justly let them serve only to determine standing between men of the same corps.

After the final examination the officers of the Engineer and Ordnance Corps would not be expected to go to sea for some years. I would have them here take a post-graduate course of eight or nine months, wholly devoted to the mechanical and physical sciences as bearing upon their life work. In this they would of course be required to attend instruction, but not to recite. An examination would be held at the end of the course, which, if satisfactory, would involve no change of rank; but failure should be followed by dropping to the following class.

The Sea Corps should similarly have a post-graduate course in the manufacture and handling of torpedoes, with such preliminary instruction in Chemistry and Electricity as may be necessary.

Having successfully passed these last named examinations the education, as far as it depends upon direct external pressure, will be finished; the rest remains with the man himself.

Their commissions as Ensigns would now be issued, and dated back to the time of the vacancies filled; provided such date should not be earlier than two years after date of graduation.

It may perhaps be not out of place to mention two advantages, not directly educational, which I hope for from this scheme.

I. Economy to the Government.

1. The total number of Midshipmen is reduced from that now existing by the number of Cadet Engineers i.e. nearly one hundred,

2. The number of officers on board ship will be diminished through all being eligible for military service. Take for example the number of officers other than surgeons, above the grade of Ensign, necessary for a ship having two divisions of guns.

In addition to which it will be remembered that in case of accident to the Engineer, who by the proposed system is an officer of the Sea Corps, his place can be filled by any one of the others. Under the existing system, the line officers not being considered capable of assuming charge of the engines, two engineers, at least, would probably be found on board a vessel of this class.

II. There would, among the officers graduated, be but one line of rank, in which each man's place would be indisputable. From whatever Corps they came they would, in joining the ship, take the quarters, duties and privileges to which their lineal rank entitled them. All would be seamen and all military men in the strict sense of the word, capable of training and commanding armed men. All would be likewise capable of assuming charge of an engine. Under these circumstances there would be good reason to hope that disputes about the right to give, or the obligation to take, orders, would largely disappear; and corps jealousies, if they still existed, would assume a form less injurious to discipline.

In conclusion of this part of my subject: It is now over a quarter of a century since the United States Naval School was founded, with a view of providing officers with better instruction than the circumstances of a ship afford; but still always with the object of making them simply better officers. Instruction, naturally and properly, has fallen into the hands of men who devote to it their whole time; or at least so large a portion of their time as to become identified with the school. This is right and necessary, for instruction is best imparted by men who thus give themselves to the business. Nevertheless, the instructor, like other men, tends to magnify his office and to mistake mental acquirements, which are simply a means, for an end. This may be bad anywhere, but, from my point of view, it is certainly and specially bad in training for a profession like the Navy, in which mere knowledge is the least of an officer's needs. Such a mistake has been gradually growing in our Naval school, and many of the younger officers of the service, under the name of science, are maintaining the idea that an extensive knowledge of mechanical processes, and an acquaintance with the elaborate mathematical reasonings involved in the investigation of problems connected with the materials placed in our hands, notably ships and ordnance, are essential to every future naval seaman. This is as unreasonable as the objections of older officers to any systematic instruction on shore. It is even worse, for it tends to substitute for a seaman's training a habit of mind and life entirely alien to it, and probably in most cases destructive of it. It is time for a reconsideration of the whole matter, and I believe that the solution is to be found in a cordial recognition of special corps, all in the line of the service, complementary of each other and not, as now, tending to mutual destruction.

II. Men.

The education of seamen must be governed by the same ultimate considerations as that of officers, viz.: What do you want to make out of the material placed in your hands?

There are two principal qualifications which are desired in every naval seaman: That he should be a seaman, and that he should be, to some degree, a gunner. In addition to these are those habits of neatness, regularity, discipline and respect for law, which we look for, but do not always find, in a man-o'-war's man.

If we are to undertake a regular system of training or education, and depend upon that for the whole, or for a chosen part, of the crews of our naval vessels, some degree of mental cultivation is necessary. It is easy, however, to exaggerate the amount desirable.

It seems evident, on the one hand, that the long periods of comparative idleness in port or even at sea, which are now too often the parents of discontent; which lead to desertion, gambling, quarrelling, rum drinking, might be made less tedious if the seaman had acquired a taste for reading books connected with his profession, with the countries he visits, or any other healthful and interesting subjects.

On the other hand it seems plain that if the Government devotes the time of the naval apprentice to acquiring knowledge above the position he is to occupy, more particularly should so use that time as to fit him for the position of an officer of a merchant vessel, it is assuring itself the disappointment of seeing its trained men leave its service for other occupations.

It is, however, neither as seamen nor as artillerists that we principally see the need of training for naval seamen. It is their moral tone that most specially calls for education and elevation.

This failure of moral tone is seen most markedly in two things. As a rule they attach no idea of moral wrong to the violation of a contract, hence desertion. Equally they have no sense of their simple dignity as men, nor of the beauty of self control, hence drunkenness unaccompanied by any sense of shame. In these two cardinal points, the two greatest evils of the Navy, they acknowledge no duty; to themselves in the last case, to others in the first.

Now I do not hope for a sudden change of sentiment and morale in a large class of men. Doubtless we must wait here for time to do its work in raising the tone of this community as it has that of others; but still the work may be hastened by persistent judicious effort to instill a sense of right and of self respect, especially if we begin with boys. The experience of more than a century has pretty well settled that severity and punishment will not stop desertion nor drunkenness. There are some who seem to think that petting will do it, while others have faith in preaching; but naval officers know pretty well that it is not necessarily the severe man who fails to gain the confidence and willing obedience of seamen, nor the indulgent coaxer that necessarily wins their good will and respect. The cause of the cheerful obedience, which one receives and another never elicits, is doubtless in that secret sympathy which the heart is quick to recognize, and which can neither be counterfeited by fair, nor concealed by harsh words. If we are to have a system of training for naval seamen, no officer should be entrusted with a share of it who is known to be one of those who "can't get work out of men," however indulgent or kind tempered he may be.

The calling and duties of a seaman are essentially of the nature of a handicraft. Quickness of eye and manual dexterity, seconded by activity and strength of the whole body, are involved in everything that he does; and very little else except native intelligence is required for making an excellent sailor. This is sufficiently shown by the admirable class of seamen of the old school, than whom no more efficient men could be found. They were intelligent doubtless—a fool will never make a sailor; but their great skill was acquired simply by practice without any pretence at education; picked up as we say. Now there can be no doubt that systematic training will produce a given result more quickly and in a greater proportionate number of instances; I am, therefore, strongly in favor of it as a means, the more so as along with the seaman's skill can be conveyed that of the artillerist, in which the men-of war's men were inferior, as well as the development of the moral and intellectual powers which will tend to make the man more trustworthy, and more capable of rational happiness, than the typical seaman of old. Still we must, as with the officer so with the man, steer clear of the mistake that each accumulation of knowledge will give the Government a better servant; which is our true end.

From what I have said, the general course I would follow can, I hope, be inferred. An apprentice system is desirable, because the lads can be more readily moulded, can more readily be attached to the service at an early age. It is not to be hoped that they can become better seamen than those of former days, but the requisite knowledge can be more quickly acquired. Ordnance is a much more complicated subject than it was; with the peculiarities and liabilities to derangement of the weapons they will have to use they should be thoroughly acquainted. As marksmen they should be as excellent as possible, though it is obvious that a man otherwise good should not be rejected for a defect here. Habits of personal cleanliness, handiness in making and caring for their own clothes, a knowledge of cooking such as will ensure both good quality and all practicable variety in the food, dancing, music, a knowledge of games, and, if there is any other thing which will tend to make ship life more enjoyable, all these should form part of their education. The radical difficulty with seamen, and above all with naval seamen, is that the life is unnatural; this must never be forgotten in considering this question of education. The difficulty is a moral one. The seaman lives without the constant solace and restraint of family life. This want, perhaps, can never be wholly supplied, but everything that tends to make up for it is a means of education to the individual and to the entire class. Combined with such provisions as the above for bodily and social enjoyment, I would provide means for healthfully occupying the mind. As all who pass through any system of apprenticeship will be taught to read. I would direct their reading as far as possible, so as to form a taste that should be not only healthy, but should coincide with the circumstances of their calling. As they will be much in foreign lands, lead them to such knowledge that they will no longer find the grog shop and the low dance house the most interesting features in a great city. Arithmetic enough to keep their accounts is good; but beyond that, time were better spent in learning languages, reading books of travel, of natural history, in short, acquiring knowledge that will enable them to enter naturally, intelligently and with interest into the life they may find around them. Devoted to a noble profession, they may find not only interest but a source of high aims and enthusiasm in naval biography and history. Novels they will read of course; but may it not be possible, in part, at least, to save their taste from falling into the yellow covered pit they now affect. In sketching this outline I don't undertake to say that all this can be done; I only claim that in the way of intellectual culture it is preferable to much that may at first glance seem more akin to our aims, as for example navigation; and I also claim that it will all tend to increase that reliability and sense of responsibility, to nourish which is, far beyond professional dexterity, the difficulty of the naval trainer. It will do this by raising the man's standard of right, and by helping to fill the void which, we must confess, a man's heart and brain do now find in the daily life of a common seaman.

Hence, to educate a body of seamen, who should form the nucleus around which our naval organization should gather, I would receive into the service a number of boys from fourteen to sixteen years of age. I do not myself attach importance to the nationality of the lad, excepting in so far as the national temperament is or is not adapted to a naval life. Other things being equal, I would reject an Irish or French lad in favor of an English, or one of the Scandinavian race; but an objection to a foreigner as such seems to me misplaced in a country so many of whose citizens are foreigners; the more so as a seaman will commonly lose sight of home ties and attach himself to the flag under which he sails. The lads thus received should be distributed in training ships, whose officers should be chosen by that practical test of being those "for whom men will work." Yet more important, if possible, than the officers, are the seamen who will be stationed on board these ships; the leaven for the lump. To my mind it would be, as a rule, a mistake to choose these from elderly seamen, however admirable their general character. Probably there is no more outrageous conservative than the ordinary old seaman; to allow such to steep a rising generation in their prejudices is simply to start that generation some twenty years behind the point at which they should begin their race. Although the character of seamen generally has advanced slowly, as compared with the progress of the world at large, still it has advanced; and the change in the main has been for the better. Let the lads then be surrounded by the best you can get, but by young men, from whom they will imbibe the best of the spirit of the age immediately preceding their own. Above all, don't make these ships the refuge of old age, however worthy.

The regulations of the department should provide against boys of vicious character being retained, as they already do against physical disability. The life should be that of a model ship of war, yet so contrived as to work in continually the systematic training by which the necessary knowledge will be steadily imparted. I mean by this that mere training is defective, unless accompanied by the daily habit of life of a real ship of war; that a special habit of life in training, differing materially from that to be pursued afterwards, is to be deprecated, unless necessary; and the necessity here seems to me to point the other way. A relatively large portion of time must, it is true, be passed in port, as the exigencies of the sea interfere too much with regularity; but I would pursue the ordinary routine of a ship of war, which affords sufficient time for the exercises of sails and guns, and instruction about them in their various details. The other portions of the day would be devoted to other instruction: marlinspike seamanship, cutting and making up clothes, cooking, carpentering, sail making, &c. Long before the period of apprenticeship has parsed, special aptitudes, when existing, will have been recognized by the officers, and it will be wise to make use of such natural bent. I do not myself see why the Engine room force should not be partially recruited in this very way as well as by direct enlistment for the purpose; and it may well be that some instruction in the engine and fire room would be of advantage to those intended mainly for the dock. My principle for officers is general instruction in all branches, special knowledge of one and I would apply the same in the end to the crew; though I am not as sure with them as with officers, that the time for so doing has fully come.

As regards the cultivation of the mind, I must adhere to my first position that the seaman is above all a handicraftsman; and that such culture as may be imparted should have for its chief object the development of manly self respect, true professional pride, and a high sense of duty; after which, and barely secondary to it, is healthful occupation for the mind, and capacity for enjoying much to which, as yet, the seaman's eye is blind. Thus surely the tone of the man will be raised, and he will be more reliable than now. In giving the various kinds of instruction alluded to, an officer, whose heart is in his work, will be careful to see that the reasons for this and that are explained. Thus, the effect of cleanliness of the person and of the ship upon health, will be pointed out as each is insisted upon; so in the carpenter's gang why one kind of lumber is good for one purpose, another for another, why one method of working up is more advantageous than another, I do not propose to lay out a program or routine in this paper; the general subjects of which I have spoken can, I feel sure, be worked in by a man of fair executive ability during the time the apprentices are with him.

The question of sending the youths out into the general service before their time is out is a difficult one. I incline to think it best not to do so at any rate before nineteen; that is, two years before the expiration of their time. Even that is over young, until the tone of the seamen in general service shall stand higher than it does now. Scruples about desertion, drunkenness, and cleanliness, beyond a certain point, would meet with too scant sympathy as yet; and I doubt whether the majority of the lads could stand against the force of the popular estimate at an early age. On the other hand, it may be urged that it is most necessary that they should have some general service, and not remain too long in leading strings. My own recommendation is to put it off as long as possible, and then try to choose your officers and crew. The entrance upon life is everywhere a critical time; how much more here, where home ties can scarcely bear, where temptation is strong, and the standard of equals generally too low.

When embarked in the service but still regarded as apprentices, care should be taken to stimulate their interest in the scenes amid which they pass, and to free their life as much as may be from the listless aimlessness in which too many seamen pass their days. But when the training ship is left, the power of choosing officers is greatly diminished; and the increase of privileges for men, such as more constant access to shore, greater command of money, and such like, must be a matter of gradual growth. However greatly we desire to see such indulgences multiplied, and however superior the ideal state for which we look, we cannot shut our eyes to the fact that progress here, as well as in other things, to be healthy must be gradual; that some officers though admirable generally, have not the knack of combining indulgence with strictness; and so, while something may be done by system and regulation, much must be left to the tact of the Commander. An impatient tendency is sometimes seen to reach desired ends by hard and fast rules, by general regulations, which cramp unduly that free action of the commanding officer upon which the efficiency of a ship must ultimately depend. It is wiser, here and everywhere, to wait for the gradual change of opinion in officers, and rise in the character of seamen, which a patient eye can surely detect now, and which will in good time bring about all that is really desirable. In any event, whatever the rule of the ship, let that, neither more nor less, be the rule for the apprentices on board her. No indulgences because they are apprentices, no keeping them as children under special evident care. Whatever their superiors may do, let it be by quiet watchfulness, by individual caution or encouragement, just such as they would extend to an older man. In a word, if being the commander or first lieutenant you wish to look out for them, don't let it be by making a special class of them, whether for care or indulgence. To do so will not only create prejudice against them among the rest of the crew, but will probably act harmfully upon themselves. The only distinction I would make would be that, being intended for seamen, they should do only seamen's duty; not messenger boy's nor berth deck cooks.

In conclusion: It has been often said that the English speaking races find their strongest motive in the sense of duty. If it be really so, it is a high privilege which those races enjoy that they respond instinctively to the noblest appeal that can be made to man; and for both officers and men it will be the task of the teacher to cherish and develop that instinct, bringing it to play not only in times of danger or hardship, to dare and to bear, but also in daily life, in little things. So men shall recognize duty not only where she calls aloud, demanding life or happiness, and all hear her; but as well in those quiet daily rounds, when her voice is so low and so monotonous that men scarcely think that duty is there at all. The man who walks daily with her and obeys her voice must be the most sure not to fail when she asks for more. Yet even to the most steadfast this path of duty is often very hard, and in it they find little sympathy; men do not recognize the difficulty, which sometimes exists mainly in the man's own nature; they know so little they can make no allowance for failures, nor appreciate the actual amount of work done. Here it is hard for man to stand alone, and yet he too often finds none to stand by him. So I think any scheme of education is defective that makes no effort to teach the learner to believe in and to depend upon God; to bear constantly about him the consciousness of one perfect friend who knows just how painful it often is to him, just how faithfully he had worked when to men he had seemed to fail; and who, however men may judge, gives credit for all and will not let seeming failure be failure in the end. The power of such a conviction is matter of history, nor, whatever may be claimed in special cases, nor, however we may be deceived by the results of natural energy and ability, do I believe an ordinary man is at his best without it. Unfortunately too many who seek to implant this reliance cannot avoid cant, the endeavor to make up for their own lack of conviction and feeling by strained words, which themselves betray their unreality; and the result is the very general discredit of an actual power. At the end of my "Essay" upon the education of these youths I urge the necessity, even as a matter of policy, of placing among them a chosen man or men who can instill into them that faith which will give completeness to their training. This, when in perfection, ensures that all the other education, all the courage, all the faculties of the man will be brought to bear on every duty placed before him; alike when unseen as when seen by men; alike in the steady, weary drag as under the stimulant of high action and danger.

CHAPTER FOUR

Leadership and Command

lthough Alfred Thayer Mahan is known for his strategic writing, and his discussion of international
grand strategy and sea power, he had a secondary
purpose for much of his writing. Mahan believed that prepar-
ing naval officers for the challenges of command was just as
vital as teaching them about strategic thought and the role of
navies in national policy. Combat leadership requires just as
much intellectual rigor as developing strategic plans. Mahan
saw his position as an early member of the U.S. Naval War
College staff as one that offered him the ability to teach naval
officers how to succeed as leaders.

As he did with most of his writing, Mahan turned to history
to find the lessons that would provide vicarious experience to
the officers he lectured. One of the places he focused was on
the history and life of Lord Admiral Horatio Nelson of the
British Royal Navy. Mahan's study of Nelson was a near constant throughout his life. In 1893, after several years serving
as an instructor at the U.S. Naval War College, Mahan was
ordered back to sea and given command of the USS *Chicago*.
He had completed a number of books, including his biography of Admiral Farragut, but he had shied away from writing
about Nelson because the subject had already been covered
by so many historians. His command of *Chicago*, however,

brought him back to England, where he met members of the Nelson family and the families of the officers who fought with him. The opportunity for research did not escape the historian in him, and Mahan was inspired. After he returned to the United States at the end of *Chicago*'s deployment, he began work on *The Life of Nelson: The Embodiment of the Sea Power of Great Britain* and worked on it from 1895 to 1897.

The book was well received by both critics and the general public, and in October of 1905 Mahan was invited to speak at Boston's Victorian Club to commemorate the hundredth anniversary of the battle of Trafalgar. He appears to have been very happy with the paper that he prepared for the lecture, and in 1908 he published it as an essay in his book *Naval Administration and Warfare: Some General Principles*. He called the essay "The Strength of Nelson."

Mahan's focus in "The Strength of Nelson" is to try and summarize the great naval officer's success and to determine what attribute contributed the most to his abilities as a combat leader. In his biography of Nelson, Mahan labeled "faith" as one of the admiral's greatest attributes. He meant faith in a secular way—faith in himself and faith in others—but was criticized by reviewers when his book was released for his apparent religious references. In his lecture before the Victorian Club he reconsidered his previous stance and said that Nelson combined the attributes of conviction, confidence, and, most of all, trust.

Readers of "The Strength of Nelson" must begin by dealing with a small amount of insecurity from the great naval historian and theorist. By way of introduction he reminds the audience that he is not James Boswell, the author of *The Life of Samuel Johnson, LL.D.*, which is considered by some to be the finest biography ever written. He stumbles through an explanation of how he approached Nelson's biography, and what his motives were. However, once he begins to delve deeply into his subject, starting with some brief anecdotes from Nelson's childhood, the leadership lesson begins.

Mahan's focus was on Nelson's sense of duty, and his trust in both others and himself. Nelson's trust in his subordinates was natural, and Mahan wrote that "this spontaneous recognition took form in an avowed scheme of life and action, which rested, consciously or unconsciously, upon the presumption in others of that same devotion to duty, that same zeal to perform it, and, in proportion to the individual's capacity, the same certainty of achievement which he found himself."[1] Nelson entered any decision, or any argument, with the assumption that the officers and men who worked for him were going to do their duty, or try their hardest. When asked by the First Lord of the Admiralty to select his own subordinate officers for a command, Nelson responded, "Choose them yourself. You cannot go amiss. The same spirit actuates the whole profession; you cannot choose wrong."[2] The admiral's trust in his men was electrifying. Those who he believed made every effort, but failed, were recognized by him with the same kind words and support as those who were successful. His men knew that if they did their duty, and if he had any control over it, Nelson would give them the recognition that they deserved.

Nelson wasn't always "good and pleasant," though. If he felt that a failure occurred because an officer or a sailor was delinquent in his duty, Mahan wrote that "his wrath had all the fierceness of trust betrayed."[3] Mahan didn't paint too rosy a picture of the admiral, writing that, "though kindly, Nelson was irritable, nervously sensitive to exasperating incidents, at times impatient to petulance, often unreasonable in complaint."[4]

Trust, however, wasn't something that was applied only to subordinates. Mahan also focused on the trust that Nelson had in himself. It was this conviction in his own decisions that allowed Nelson to face risk. He was a firm believer in taking risks, because only with risk came reward. Nelson realized he wasn't infallible, but he also knew that doubt and indecision would destroy an officer's ability to make command decisions. In "The Strength of Nelson," Mahan recognized some failing in himself, admitting that at times he had worked through a problem reasonably and had come to a course of action, "but [had] not the nerve to take [it] because of the remaining doubt. Here reason, the goddess of to-day, halts and fails."[5]

Combat leadership faces many new challenges in the twenty-first century. The rapid expansion of information technology and the rise of the networked battlefield has created a temptation for many senior officers to become more involved at the tactical level. P. W. Singer has written about this phenomenon as "The Rise of the Tactical General."[6] The challenge that it creates for good combat decisionmaking and leadership is a challenge based on trust. As military forces become more nimble, and hybrid and asymmetric conflicts create environments where rapid decisionmaking is vital, the central role of trust in leadership and command is as important today as it was a century ago when Mahan wrote about it, and a century before that when Nelson practiced it.

THE STRENGTH OF NELSON[7]

August 1905

With a temperament versatile as that of Nelson, illustrated in a career full of varied action, it is not easy to know how to regard its subject, in brief, so as to receive a clear and accurate impression; one which shall preserve justice of proportion, while at the same time giving due emphasis and predominance to the decisive characteristics. Multiplicity of traits, lending itself to multiplicity of expression, increases the difficulty of selection, and of reproducing that combination which really constitutes the effective force and portrait of the man. The problem is that of the artist, dealing with a physical exterior. We can all recall instances of persons, celebrated historically or socially, in whom the prominence of a particular feature, or a certain pervading expression, causes all portraits to possess a recognizable stamp of likeness. As soon as the pictured face is seen we identify the original without hesitation. There are others in whom the mobility of countenance, the variations depending upon feeling and expression, quite overpower in impression the essential sameness presented by features in repose.

Great indeed must be the difficulties of the artist, or the writer, who has to portray the man capable, within a half-hour, of such diverse moods as Wellington witnessed in his one only interview with Nelson. The anecdote is too familiar for reproduction here. Less well known, probably, or less remembered, is a similar testimony borne by two officers, Captains Layman and Sir Alexander Ball, who served with him under varying circumstances.

One day, after tea in the drawing-room at Merton, Lord Nelson was earnestly engaged in conversation with Sir Samuel Hood. Mr. Layman observed to Sir Alexander that Lord Nelson was at work, by his countenance and mouth; that he was a most extraordinary man, possessing opposite points of character—little in little things, but by far the greatest man in great things he ever saw; that he had seen him petulant in trifles, and as cool and collected as a philosopher when surrounded by dangers in which men of common minds with clouded countenance would say, "Ah! what is to be done?" It was a treat to see his animated and collected countenance in the heat of action. Sir Alexander remarked this seeming inconsistency, and mentioned that after the Battle of the Nile the captains of the squadron were desirous to have a good likeness of their heroic chief taken, and for that purpose employed one of the most eminent painters in Italy. The plan was to ask the painter to breakfast, and get him to begin immediately after. Breakfast being over, and no preparation being made by the painter, Sir Alexander was selected by the other captains to ask him when he intended to begin; to which the answer was, "Never." Sir Alexander said he stared, and they all stared, but the artist continued: "There is such a mixture of humility with ambition in Lord Nelson's countenance that I dare not risk the attempt!"

Contrast with such an one the usual equable composure of Washington or Wellington, and the difficulty of a truthful rendering is seen; but reflection reveals therein likewise the intensely natural, spontaneous, impulsive character, which takes hold of our loves, and abides in affectionate remembrance.

In such cases how can there but be marked diversities of appearance in the attempted reproductions by this or that man, painter or writer? Not only will the truthfulness of the figured face depend upon the fleeting mood of the sitter; the aptitude of the artist to receive, and to penetrate through the mask of the instant, is an even greater factor. Both the one and the other will enter into the composition of the resultant portrait; for as, on the one hand, the man shows himself as he for the moment is, so, on the other, the power to see and to express that which is shown depends upon the revelation to the artist; a revelation due as much to his own insight as to the visible thing before him. The miracle of Pentecost lay not only in the gifts of speech bestowed upon the Apostles, but in the power of every man to hear in that tongue, and in that tongue only, to which he is born; to see with the spiritual vision which he has received, or to which he may have grown.

In this respect portrayal by pen will not differ from portrayal by pencil or by brush. The man who attempts to depict in words a character so diverse in manifestation as that of Nelson will reflect from what he sees before him that aspect of the man with which he himself is most in touch. The writer of military sympathies will—must—give predominance to the military qualities. Despite his efforts to the contrary, they will make the deepest impress, and will be most certainly and conspicu-ously reproduced. And to a degree this will accord with the truth; for above all, undoubtedly, Nelson was a warrior. But he was also much more, and in virtue of that something else he survives, and is transmitted to us as—what shall I say?—as Nelson; there is no other word. He is not a type; still less does he belong to a class. He is simply himself—the man Nelson; a man so distinct in his individuality, that he has thus imposed himself on the consciousness and recollection of a great nation. He rests there, simply himself, and no other; and no other is he, nor stands near him. I say not that he is higher or lower, greater or less, than any other. I do not, at least now, analyze his qualities, nor seek to present such an assembly of them as shall show why the impress of individuality is thus unique. I only draw attention to the fact that this is so; that Nelson now lives, and is immortal in the memory of his kind, not chiefly because of what he did, but because in the doing and in the telling, then and now, first and last, men have felt themselves in the presence of a personality so strong that it has broken through the barriers of convention and reserve which separate us one from another, and has placed itself in direct con-tact with the inner selves, not of contemporaries only, but of us who never saw him in the body. We have not only heard of him and his deeds. We know him as we do one with whom we are in constant intercourse.

This is of itself an extraordinary trait. Thus to make a man known, to reveal a personality, is what Boswell did for Johnson; but he accom-plished this literary marvel of portraiture by the most careful and minute record of doings and sayings. His is a built-up literary prodigy, resem-bling some of those striking Flemish portraits, which not only impress by their *ensemble*, but stand inspection under a magnifying glass. But what Boswell did for Johnson, Nelson has done for himself, and in quite other fashion. He is revealed to us, not by such accumulation of detail, but by some quality, elusive, perhaps not to be detected, by reason of which the man himself insensibly transpires to our knowledge in his strength and in his weakness. We know him, not by what his deeds or his words signify; but through his deeds and words the inner spirit of the man continually pierces, and, while we read, envelops us in an atmosphere which may be called Nelsonic. Such certainly seemed to me the effect upon myself in a year given to his letters, to his deeds, and to his recorded words. I found myself in a special environment, stimulating, exalting, touching; and while we confess that there are morbid symptoms attendant upon the writing of biography, tending to distort vision, and to confuse the sense of proportion, faults which the reader must appreciate—the writer cannot—there can be no mistake about the moral effect produced, and the outburst of this Trafalgar Day proves it to be not limited to the biographer. The reserve which for the most of us cloaks each man's secret being from the knowledge of those nearest him among his contemporaries, casts no such impenetrable veil over the personality of this man whom we never saw—who died just one hundred years ago this day. We have with him an acquaintance, we feel from him an influence, which we have not with, nor from, one in a score of those whom we meet daily.

Many Lives of Nelson have been written, but no one of them marked with the artistic skill and untiring diligence which Boswell brought to his task. A singular proof of the latter's combined genius and care, which I do not think is always appreciated, is to be found in the fact that the portrait of Johnson is surrounded by a gallery of minor portraits, as real and living as his own, though duly subordinated in impression to the central figure of the group. This is indeed the triumph of the great artist. He has, so to say, succeeded beyond himself, and beyond his intentions, simply because he *is* great. In the way of portraiture he touches nothing that he does not quicken and adorn. The same certainly cannot be said for those who have transmitted to us the companions of Nelson, in their relations to their chief. Yet we know Nelson as well as we know Johnson, and more usefully, despite every disadvantage in his limners. The spell of his personality has compelled them to reproduce him; and its power—its magic, I might say—is to be found in that influence exerted upon them. In Boswell's Johnson we have the vivid reproduction of a man of the past; a study complete, interesting, instructive, but not to a reader of to-day influential beyond the common teachings of biography. In Nelson, who died but twenty years later, we have a living inspiration. He presents a great heroic standard, a pattern. We set ourselves at once to copy him; not because, in the record of his acts, we have received an ordinary suggestion or warning, but because heart answers to heart. The innate nobility of the man's ideals, which transpired even through, and in, the lamentable episode which sullied his career, uplifts us in spite of ourselves, and of all that was amiss in him. The jewel shines, even amid defilement. It certainly cannot be claimed that Nelson's unflinching professional tenacity is nobler than Johnson's brave struggle against his mental depression and numerous bodily infirmities; his life unstained, though without Puritanic affectation. But, as a present force, Johnson is dead, Nelson is alive. Nelson is no mere man of the past. Not his name only, but he himself lives to us; still speaks, because there was in him that to which man can never die, while he remains partaker of the Divine nature. It is but a few days since that I received a letter from a junior officer of the British Navy, expressing the wish that all young officers might be ordered to master the career of Nelson, because of the uplifting power which he himself had found in the ideals and actions of the hero.

What is the secret of this strange fascination, which has given Nelson his peculiar place, by which it may be said of him, as of some few other worthies of the past: "He being dead yet speaketh." It certainly is not merely in the standards which he professed, even although his devotion to them continually was manifested, not in word only, but in deed; yea, and in the hour of death. The noblest of all, the dying words, "Thank God I have done my duty," is no monopoly of Nelson's. You may count by scores the men of English-speaking tradition, in Great Britain and America, who have brought as single-minded a purpose to the service of the "stern daughter of the voice of God," and have followed her as unflinchingly through good and ill. But how many of them who have departed exercise a conscious influence upon the minds of the men of to-day? Their deeds and examples doubtless have gone to swell that sum total of things, by which the world of our generation is the better for the lives of the myriads who have lived unknown and are forgotten; but their influence, their present, direct, personal, uplifting force on men now alive, in how many instances can you point to it? And to what one other, among the heroes of Great Britain, from whom it is so generally distributed that it may fitly be called national? Despite the Nile and Trafalgar, there may be several who have more radically and permanently affected the destinies of the Empire. We are not here concerned with such analytic computations, or with estimates of indirect consequences which the doer of the deeds could by no possibility have foreseen. If such there be, what one among them evokes to-day the emulative affection and admiration which is the prerogative of Nelson? Whence comes this? Grant even the cumulative dramatic force, the immense effectiveness of the double utterances, so closely following each other, "England expects every man to do his duty," and "Thank God, I have done *my* duty," you have advanced but a step towards the solution of the question. Why is Nelson still alive, while so many other sons of duty are dead? What prophetic power, power to speak for God and for man, was in this man, that such enduring speech should come forth from his life; that he, being dead, is still speaking?

It is not permitted to man so to search the heart of his fellow as to give a conclusive reply to such a question; yet it is allowable and appropriate to seek so far to appreciate one like Nelson as at least to approach somewhat nearer towards understanding the secret of his character and of its power. The homage to duty as the supreme motive in life, and the strong conviction that there are objects worthier of effort than money getting and ease, were characteristics possessed in common with many others by Nelson. But, while I speak with diffidence, I feel strongly that the mode of tenure was somewhat different in him and in them. The recognition of duty, and of its high obligation, is impressed upon most of us from without. We have been taught it, have received it by the hearing of the ear, from others to whom in like manner it has been imparted by those who went before them. It is, so to say, a transmitted inheritance—"in the air;" perhaps not to quite such an extent as might be desired. We render it a tribute which is perfectly sincere, but still somewhat conventional. This condition is not to be despised. The compelling power of accepted conventions is enormous; but, like much religious faith, such attention to duty is not founded on the individual bottom, but depends largely on association, for which reason it will be found more highly developed in some professions, because it is the tone of the profession. Unquestionably, in many individuals the thought is so thoroughly assimilated as to become the man's very own, as hard to depart from as any ingrained acquired habit; and to this we owe the frequency of its manifestations in nations where the word itself has received a dignity of recognition which sets it apart from the common vocabulary—deifies it, so to say.

All this is very fine. It is superb to see human nature, in man or in people, lifting itself up above itself by sheer force of adhesion to a great ideal; to mark those who have received the conception elevated, not through their own efforts, but by force of association, like the tonic effect of an invigorating atmosphere. But our hard-won victories over ourselves cannot by themselves alone make us that which by nature we are not. Nature has been suppressed in its evil, and upon its restless revolt good enthroned; but the evil lives still and rebels. The palace is kept and held by a strong man armed; but ever in danger that a stronger than he, whom we call Nature, shall return in force and retrieve his past defeat. It was finely said of Washington, by one who knew him intimately—Gouverneur Morris—"Control his passions! Yes; and few men have had stronger to control. But many men have controlled their passions, so as not to do that to which they were impelled. But where have you known one who, like him, always, under whatever conditions, could do, and did, what the duty of the moment required, despite fatigue, or distaste, or natural repulsion." The writer who made this comparison had moved amid all the scenes of dire distress and anxiety that marked the American War of Independence, and had personal acquaintance with the chief actors. This is the innate positive quality, not the acquired negative self-control, battling with self. I doubt if most of us stop to realize the full force of the word "innate," which slips glibly enough from our tongues without appreciation of its significance. Inborn; this is not nature controlled, but nature controlling; not the tiger, or the ape, or the sloth, held by the throat, but the man himself in the fullness of his powers exercising his natural supremacy over himself. Such was duty to Nelson; a mistress, not that compelled obedience, but that attracted the devotion of a nature which intuitively recognised her loveliness, and worshipped. Like the hearers at Pentecost, he recognized in her voice the tongue to which he was born; he saw her—yes, despite his one great fall, we may say it—he saw her fairer than the daughters of men.

> *Stern Lawgiver! Thou dost wear*
> *The Godhead's most benignant grace;*
> *Nor know we anything so fair*
> *As is the smile upon thy face.*

A natural character, we have all felt the attractiveness of such, the attractiveness of truth and beauty; but when, to such a nature, is added nobility as well, we have one of the rare combinations which compels homage. Nelson was eminently natural, affectionate, impulsive, expansive; but it is this singular gift, this peculiar recognition of duty, with another I shall mention, which has set him upon his pedestal, given him the niche which only he can fill. In the spirits of his people he has found a nobler Westminster Abbey than that of which he dreamed. But, you may ask, how do you demonstrate that he had this gift? Alas, I am not a Boswell; I wish I were, and that there survived the records of conversations with which I, or another, could reconstruct his image, as Boswell drew Johnson. Yet when a career opens and closes upon the same keynote, we may be sure of the harmonious whole—of which, indeed, traces enough remain to confirm our assurances. You know the two stories of childhood handed down to us. The brothers starting for school after Christmas holidays, driven back by the weather, and started again with the father's mandate, "You may return if it is necessary; but I leave it to your honor not to do so unless it is really dangerous to proceed." It seemed dangerous, and one was for returning; but Nelson said, "No, it was left to our honor." Not the word "duty," no; but the essence of duty, the look out from self, the recognition of the something external and higher than the calls of the body. In one so young—he was but twelve when he went to sea some time after this—it is Nature which speaks, not an acquired standard. In later years, in terms somewhat fantastic, he said he beheld ever a radiant orb beckoning him onward. Honor he called it, the twin sister—rather let us say the express image—in which duty, regarding as in a glass, sees herself reflected. Then, again, there is the story of stealing the fruit from the schoolmaster's pear-tree—a trivial enough schoolboy prank, risking the penalties of detection which his comrades dared not face. Neither duty nor honor goes to such a feat in its nakedness; but the refusal to eat the fruit, the proud avowal that he went only because the others feared, bears witness to the same disregard of personal advantage, the same determination of action by consider-ations external to self, the same eye to the approval of the conscious-ness—of the conscience—which spoke in the signal at Trafalgar, and soothed the dying moments by the high testimony within: not, "I have won renown;" not "I have achieved success;" but, "I have done my duty." He was not indifferent to success; he was far from indifferent to renown. "If it be a sin to covet glory," he once quoted, "then am I the most offending soul alive." But the solemn hour which gives the validity of an oath to the statement of the dying, assuredly avouches to us that then the man, as once the child, spoke out the true secret of his being—the tongue into which he was born.

And in this also is the secret, not only of his own devotion to duty, but of the influence of his personality upon others; both in the infancy of his professional career, and now in the maturity of his immortal renown. What he thus possessed he possessed naturally, positively, aggressively, and therefore contagiously. He had root in himself, to use a familiar expression; and the life which was thus no mere offshoot of convention, but his very own, gave itself out abundantly to others, multiplying him-self. He gave out by example; he gave out by words, uttered, indeed, expressly, yet so casually that the impression resembles the fleeting glimpse of an interior, caught through the momentary tossing aside of a curtain; he gave out through the heroic atmosphere of self-devotion which he bore about him; he gave out by cordial recognition of excellence in others. Any other man who did his duty, whether comrade or subordinate, was to him a fellow worshipper at the shrine; his heart went out to him, whether in failure or in success, if only the will was there. No testimony is clearer or more universal than that to his generosity in appreciation of others; and it was seen, not only in recognition of achievement already accomplished, but in the confident expectation of achievement yet to be effected. The original form of the Trafalgar signal, spoken by himself, "Nelson *confides* that every man will do his duty," was no mere casual utterance. It summed up the conviction and habit of a lifetime. As the words, "Thank God, I have done my duty," were his dying words personally, so those just quoted may be said to have been his last words professionally. Indeed, he himself said as much, for when they had been communicated to the fleet he remarked, "Now I can do no more. We must trust (confide) to the great Disposer of all events." His great career ended when that signal had been read and acknowledged.

Because in himself so trustworthy, he trusted abundantly; and all of us know the stimulus of feeling ourselves trusted, of looking forward with certainty to just appreciation of good work done. "I am well aware," wrote one of his younger captains, "of the good construction which your Lordship has ever been in the habit of putting on circumstances, although wearing the most unfavorable appearances. Your Lordship's good opinion constitutes the summit of my ambition and the most effective spur to my endeavors." "I am pleased," writes another, "that an opportunity is offered for showing my gratitude in a small degree for his almost fatherly kindness." In a letter of instructions to a captain about to encounter some perplexing and critical conditions, after prescribing for several circumstances that may arise, he concludes, in the case of the unforeseen, "You must then act as your judgment may direct you, and *I am sure* that will be very proper." If delinquency actually occurred, as he conceived it had in the case of Sir Sidney Smith, his wrath had all the fierceness of trust betrayed, for he was a man impatient and of strong passions; but otherwise doubts of another's doing his duty did not occur to him. His confidence in himself, in his own self-devotion and capacity, made him trustful of others, and inspired them with devotion to the service and to the country, for his sake, and because they saw it in him. A captain who met him for the first time just before Trafalgar, and who fell in the battle, wrote home, "I have been very lucky with most of my admirals, but I really think the present the pleasantest I have met with. He is so good and pleasant that we all wish to do what he likes, without any kind of orders."

This was the clear reflection of his own spirit, begot of his own confidence in others, because he met them and trusted them as himself. Dutiful, probably, in any event, as imitators of him they were more so. He expected in others what he felt in himself, and diffused around him the atmosphere of energy, zeal, and happiness in endeavor, which was native to himself. "He had in a great degree," wrote a contemporary who had known him from boyhood, "the valuable but rare quality of conciliating the most opposite tempers, and forwarding the public service with unanimity, among men not of themselves disposed to accord." Yes; but the unanimity was not that of accordant opinion, but of a common devotion to a common object, before which differences subsided; to duty, seeing in others a like devotion, a like purpose to do their best. This spirit Nelson shed about him; with this he inspired others in his day, and still does in our own. It was the contagion of his personality, continuous in action, and ever watchful against offence, and even against misunderstanding. "My dear Keats," he wrote to a captain whose worn out ship was incorrigibly slow when speed was most desirable, "I am fearful you may think that the *Superb* does not go as fast as I could wish. I would have you to be assured that I know and feel that the *Superb* does all which is possible for a ship to accomplish; and I desire that you will not fret." "My dear Collingwood, I shall come out and make you a visit; not, my dear friend, to take your command from you, but *to consult* how we may best serve our country by detaching a part of this large force." St. Vincent's testimony here is invaluable: "The delicacy you have always shown to senior officers is a sure presage of your avoiding by every means in your power to give umbrage." He wrote himself, "If ever I feel great, it is in never having, in thought, word, or deed, robbed any man of his fair fame."

Instances of this delicate consideration for the feelings of others, dictated often by appreciation of their temperaments as well as of their circumstances, could be multiplied. But we read them imperfectly, missing their significance, if we see in them mere kindliness of temper; for, though kindly, Nelson was irritable, nervously sensitive to exasperating incidents, at times impatient to petulance, often unreasonable in complaint. Open expression of these feelings, evidences of temperament, flit often across his countenance, traversing the unity of the artist's vision and embarrassing his conception. Nelson was not faultless; but he was great. It is not, indeed, unprecedented to find such foibles in connection with much kindliness; they are easy concomitants in a warm temper. But this appreciation and consideration were with him no mere kindliness of temper, though that entered into them. They were the reflection outward of that which he knew and experienced within. In his followers he saw himself. To use the quaint expression of Swedenborg, he projected around him his own sphere. Because duty, zeal, energy inspired him, he saw them quickening others also; and the homage he intuitively paid to those qualities themselves he gave to their possessors whom he saw around him. Each man, unless proved recreant, thus stood transfigured in the light which came from Nelson's self. This spontaneous recognition took form in an avowed scheme of life and action, which rested, consciously or unconsciously, upon the presumption in others of that same devotion to duty, that same zeal to perform it, and, in proportion to the individual's capacity, the same certainty of achievement which he found in himself. "Choose them yourself," he replied to the First Lord of the Admiralty, when asked to name his officers. "You cannot go amiss. The same spirit actuates the whole profession; you cannot choose wrong."

The man to whose lips such words rise spontaneous simply attributes to others what he finds within, and what by experience he has found himself able to transfer. Out of the abundance of the heart he speaks, and by his words he is justified.

Closely connected with this characteristic, as is warp with woof, interwoven manifestation indeed of a quality essentially one and the same, is a trait in Nelson upon which I myself have been inclined to lay an emphasis which I do not find in other writers. So far as analysis can draw lines between the essential features of a particular character, the one to which I now allude is peculiarly military in its effectiveness; whereas devotion to duty, and confidence in others, may rather be called personal. At least they are not to be attributed exclusively to the military professions, much as these undoubtedly have gained from the insistence, approaching monopoly, with which in them the idea of duty has been enforced, as supreme among the incentives of the soldier. To the Happy Warrior, Duty does not bar devotion to other virtues, except in rivalry with herself. Courage, obedience, fortitude, Duty recognizes them all and admits them; but not as equals. They are but parts of herself; the children, not the mother. Differing one from another, in her they find that which unites and consecrates them all. But while from all Duty exacts much, there are gifts which she cannot confer; and among them is one found in few, but conspicuous in Nelson.

In my own attempt to deal with his career, I spoke of this as Faith; and the word was criticized as inadequate and misleading, apparently because I was thought to use it in a narrowly religious sense. Now, I do not think that Nelson would have rejected religious trust in God as a prime motive in his professional action; but certainly, to my mind, if Jesus Christ spoke with only the authority of a man, he expressed a profound philosophy when He placed faith at the foundation of all lofty and successful action, religious or other. But while faith has a recognized technical meaning in theology, it has a much wider practical application; and when called confidence, or conviction, it is more easy to understand its value in the perplexities, the doubtful circumstances, which go to make all life, but especially the life of the military leader, responsible for great issues, such as fell to Nelson's determination. Then conviction, when possessed, becomes indeed the solid substance of things which the man cannot see with his eyes, nor know by ordinary knowledge. It is the bed-rock upon which action rears its building, and stands four square against all the winds that blow. It is not so much a possession as that the man is possessed by it, and goes forward; not knowing whither he goes, but sure that, wherever the path leads, he does right to follow. As Nelson trusted his fellows, so he trusted the voice within, and for the same reason; in both he recognized the speech to which he was born.

Most of us know what it is to be tossed to and fro by hesitations, and thereby too often deterred from action, or weakened in it. Can any one who has felt this inward anguish, and the feebleness of suspense, and at last has arrived at a working certainty, doubt the value and power of a faculty which reaches such certainty, reaches conviction, by processes which, indeed, are not irrational, but yet in their influence transcend reason? How clearly does reason sometimes lead us step by step to a conclusion so probable as to be worthy of being called a practical certainty, and there leave to our unaided selves the one further, step to acceptance; the step across the chasm which yawns between conviction and knowledge, between faith and sight. This we have not the nerve to take because of the remaining doubt. Here reason, the goddess of to-day, halts and fails. The leap to acceptance, which faith takes, and wins, reason cannot make, nor is it within her gift to man. The consequent weakness and failure are more conspicuous in military life than in any other, because of the greatness of the hazards, the instancy and gravity of the result, should acceptance bring disaster. The track of military history is strewn with the dead reputations and the shattered schemes which have failed to receive the quickening element of conviction.

Of all inborn qualities, this is one of the strongest, as it is the rarest; for, let it be marked, such conviction consists, not in the particular conclusion reached, but in the dominating power with which it is held. This puts out of court all other considerations before entertained—but now cast aside—and acts; acts as though no other conclusion were possible, or ever had been. This to me has always invested with the force of a most profound allegory the celebrated incident of Nelson putting the glass to his blind eye, when looking at the signal which contravened his conviction. The time for hesitations had passed; there had been a time for discussion, but there remained now but one road to success. Conviction shuts its eyes to all else; the man who admits doubts at such an instant is lost. It is again single-mindedness, the single eye, the undoubting, revealed amid new surroundings. Conviction is one; doubts many. At the moment of this sublime exhibition, the words of the bystander depict Nelson as one breathing inspiration: "Though the fire of the enemy had slackened, the result had certainly not declared in favor on either side. Nelson was sometimes animated, and at others heroically fine in his observations. "It is warm work, and this day may be the last for any of us at a moment; but mark you, I would not be elsewhere for thousands." "Leave off action! D— me if I do." The man was possessed, in the noble sense of the word.

With less dramatic force, but no less telling and decisive effect, the same power of conviction manifested itself in a peculiarly critical moment of his career, near the close of his life. In May, 1805, he left his station in the Mediterranean to pursue an allied fleet to the West Indies. He had done this without other authority than his own inferences from the data before him; yielding, to quote a French admirer, to one of the finest inspirations of his genius. The West Indies reached, he failed to get touch of the enemy, owing to misinformation given him; and they started back to Europe, leaving no certain trace of where they were gone. Opinions and rumors clamored and clattered around him; certainty could not be had. He has recorded the situation himself in words which convey, more forcibly than my pen can, what is the power of conviction. "So far from being infallible, like the Pope, I believe my opinions to be very fallible, and therefore I may be mistaken that the enemy's fleet has gone to Europe; *but I cannot bring myself to think otherwise*, notwithstanding the variety of opinions which different people *of good judgment* form." "My opinion is *firm as a rock*, that some cause has made them resolve to proceed direct for Europe." Can conviction use stronger words?

And what is conviction but trust; trust in the unseen? Trust not irrational, not causeless, not unable to give some account of itself; but still short of knowledge, ignorant in part, deriving its power, not from what it sees, but from an unseen source within. To deny the existence and strength of such a faculty in some favored men is to shut one's eyes to the experience of history, and of daily life around us; a blindness, or a perversity, quite as real as it would be to ignore the shilly-shally vacillations of the multitude of clever men, who never find in themselves the power to act upon their opinions, if action involves risk, because opinion receives not that inward light which we called conviction, confidence, trust, faith. In Nelson this confidence, like his devotion to duty, and his trust in others, envelops his record, like an atmosphere which one insensibly feels, but the power of which is realized only by stopping to reflect. Lord Minto, who had known him intimately from the very beginnings of his greatness, and who knew the navy too, wrote after his death: "The navy is certainly full of the bravest men; but there was a sort of heroic cast about Nelson that I never saw in any other man, and which seems wanting to the achievement of *impossible things*, which became easy to him." Not that he had not to encounter perplexities and doubts in plenty. There is little singularity in conviction where there is nothing to shake it. None of us have trouble in admitting that two and two make four. But as Nelson's actions are followed, whatever the obscurity of the conditions, one finds oneself always in presence of a spirit as settled in its course, when once decided, as though doubt were not possible.

Our quest has been the strength of Nelson. I find it in the inborn natural power to trust; to trust himself and others; to confide, to use his own word. Whether it is the assurance within, which we call conviction, or the assurance without, which we call confidence, in others or in one's own action, this is the basic principle and motive force of his career, as Duty was its guiding light and controlling standard. I make less of his clear perceptions, his sound judgment, of the general rational processes which illuminated his course, as I also do of the courage, fortitude, zeal, which illustrated his deeds. All these things, valuable as they are, he shared with others. He possessed them, possibly, in an unusual degree, but still in common with many to whom they could never bring success, because unassociated with that indefinable something, which, like a yet undiscovered element in nature, or an undetected planet, we recognize by its workings, and may to it even attribute a name, though unable as yet adequately to describe. Genius, we not infrequently say; a word which, not yet defined, stands a mute confession of our ignorance wherein it consists. As I conceive it, there is no genius greater than faith; though it may well be that in so saying we have but given another name with no nearer approach to a definition.

In a celebrated funeral oration, which we all know, the speaker says: "I come to bury Caesar, not to praise him." It is for no such purpose that men observe this day; for the man, the memory of whom now moves his people, is not one to be buried, but to be praised and kept in everlasting remembrance. True, he needs not our praises, but we need to praise him for our own sakes. The Majesty on high is exalted far above all praise, yet it is good to praise Him; for the essence of praise is not the homage of the lips, but the recognition of excellence; and recognition, when real, elevates, ennobles. It fosters an ideal which tends to induce imitation, and to uplift by sheer force of appreciation and association. And as with the Creator, so with the excellent among his creatures. We need not ignore their failings, or their sins, although an occasion like the present is not one for dwelling upon these; but as we recognize in them men of like frailties with ourselves, we yet perceive that, despite all, they have not only done the great works, but have been the great men whom we may justly reverence. That they in their weakness have had so much in common with us gives hope that we may yet have something in common with them in their strength. It is the high grace and privilege of a man like Nelson that he provokes emulation rather than rivalry, imitation rather than competition. To extol him uplifts ourselves. As it was when he lived on earth, so it is now. His life is an inheritance to children's children; of his own people first, but after them of all the nations of the earth.

CHAPTER FIVE

_____

History and Conventional Wisdom

I n 1901 Mahan finished a collection of short biographies titled *Types of Naval Officers: Drawn from the History of the British Navy.* His purpose in writing the volume was to illuminate leadership styles and operational specialties, and demonstrate that together each had an important contribution to the hegemony developed by the Royal Navy. He wrote that "the Navy tends to, and for efficiency requires, specialization." Mahan's biography of Edward Pellew, who would earn the title of Lord of Exmouth after Britain's victory over Napoleon, provides readers with an example from his writing that challenges the way in which he is commonly taught. If Mahan was only interested in the battleships or the main battlefleet, in big guns and large maneuvering forces, why would he write the biography of an officer who spent the vast majority of his very successful career in frigates, both as a junior officer and as a commander?

Pellew began his career with a direct link to American naval history, fighting on Lake Champlain during the War of Independence. He rapidly developed a reputation as a junior officer of great courage and daring. His example of courage, as well as technical expertise, was an inspiration to sailors as the British built their flotilla to face Benedict Arnold's American forces. Mahan highlights the importance of a dynamic personality, and the willingness to take risk, as important developmental stages for a junior officer who will be promoted to command. Here, in the wilderness, helping to build a gunboat fleet, Mahan finds valuable examples of naval excellence despite the fact that it is about as far from a ship-of-the-line as a sailor or officer could get.

Pellew's biography is full of examples like his service on the American frontier. At the end of his career, the admiral's final operation involved the decades-long conflict with the Barbary pirates that was fought by a number of navies from Europe, as well as the United States. In 1816 the British government decided, with the victory over Napoleon still fresh, that it was time to end the piracy of the Barbary territories once and for all.

Pellew, then in command of the Mediterranean, and his battlefleet were dispatched to the coast of Algeria. Mahan highlights this mission despite the fact that there was no intention to face another battlefleet, and that Pellew's force was sent to address what we today would consider an irregular threat or hybrid challenge. The British rendezvoused with a Dutch fleet, and Pellew took command of a combined force that sailed into the port at Algiers and demanded the release of all Europeans held by the Barbary territories as slaves and hostages. When their demand was refused, the combined force bombarded the city of Algiers, destroying the forces of the pasha and resulting in the release of the hostages and the end of attacks from the North African principalities. Mahan valued Pellew's mission, and his execution of it, as an example not only of British power projection, but also of multinational naval cooperation. Neither type of operation is commonly associated with being "Mahanian."

Mahan used his writing of history to illuminate principles and examples that were important for naval officers. By understanding and learning from these examples, it would help ensure their own successes. Historian Jon Sumida has suggested that "the crucial linkages between his past and our present, in other words, are not to be found in his conclusions but in his questions and his conduct of the inquiry."[1] Mahan's choice to write about Pellew demonstrates that he recognized the place in naval warfare for non-traditional missions, service detached from the main battlefleet, and what he called "partisan" service. He wrote that "this independent but yet restricted sphere afforded the fullest scope for a conspicuous display of those splendid qualities—fearlessness, enterprise, sound judgment, instant decision, and superb seamanship—which he so eminently possessed." Mahan wrote numerous times about the importance of a fleet made up of more than just the main battlefleet of heavy battleships. Pellew's biography offered him the opportunity to show the importance of cruisers, on detached service or in small squadrons, which could range the world's oceans and fulfill their nation's missions. Reading *Pellew: The Frigate Captain and Partisan Officer* provides students, sailors, and officers in the twenty-first century a chance to experience some of Mahan's historical writing, while also learning that the strategist and instructor considered service outside of the main battlefleet as valuable and vital to naval success.

PELLEW: THE FRIGATE CAPTAIN AND PARTISAN OFFICER

1757–1833

Like the English tongue itself, the names of British seamen show the composite origin of their nation. As the Danes after the day of Copenhagen, to them both glorious and disastrous, claimed that in Nelson they had been vanquished by a man of their own blood, descended from their Viking forefathers; as Collingwood and Troubridge indicate the English descent of the two closest associates of the victor of Trafalgar; so Saumarez and the hero of this sketch, whose family name was Pellew, represent that conquering Norman race which from the shores of the Northern ocean carried terror along the coasts of Europe and the Mediterranean, and as far inland as their light keels could enter. After the great wars of the French Revolution and the Battle of Algiers, when Lord Exmouth had won his renown and his position had been attained, kinship with him was claimed by a family still residing in Normandy, where the name was spelled "Pelleu." Proof of common origin was offered, not only in the name, but also in the coat of arms.

In England, the Pellew family was settled in the extreme southwest, in Cornwall and Devonshire, counties whose nearness to the great Atlantic made them the source of so much of the maritime enterprise that marked the reign of Elizabeth. Lord Exmouth's grandfather was a man of wealth; but, as he left many children, the juniors had to shift for themselves, and the youngest son, Samuel Pellew, the father of the admiral, at the time of the latter's birth commanded a post-office packet on the Dover station. He accordingly made the town of that name the home of his wife and children; and there Edward, the second of his four sons, was born, April 19, 1757. Their mother was the daughter of a Jacobite gentleman, who had been out for the Pretender in 1715—a fact which probably emphasized the strong Hanoverian sympathies of Samuel Pellew, whose habit was to make his children, every Sunday, drink King George's health upon their knees.

In 1765, when the future admiral was only eight years old, his father died, and the mother making an imprudent marriage three years later, the children were thrown upon the world with small provision and scanty care. The resolute, active, and courageous character of the lads, however, brought them well forward among their equals in age. At school Edward was especially distinguished for fearlessness. Of this he gave a marked instance, when not yet twelve, by entering a burning house where gunpowder was stored, which no other of the bystanders would approach. Alone and with his own hands the lad brought out the powder. A less commendable but very natural result of the same energetic spirit was shown in the numerous fighting matches in which he was engaged. Being threatened with a flogging for one of these, the circumstance became the immediate occasion of his going to sea. If flogged, he declared, he would run away; and as a decided taste for seafaring life had already manifested itself, his guardian thought better to embrace at once the more favorable alternative and enter him regularly in the navy. He thus went afloat towards the end of 1770, the date at which Nelson, also, though one year younger, began his career.

His first cruise was in the Mediterranean. It came to a premature end through a quarrel between the commander of the ship and one of the midshipmen. In this the captain was clearly and grossly in the wrong; yet nevertheless carried his resentment, and the power of oppression in his hands, then little restrained by law, so far as to expel the youngster from the ship and set him on shore in Marseilles. Pellew insisted upon accompanying his messmate, and the two lads of fourteen, aided by some of the lieutenants, secured a passage home. It shows a pleasing trait in our hero's character that, some years afterwards, he advanced materially the professional fortunes of the son of the officer who had thus abused his authority.

He next passed under the command of a Captain Pownoll, between whom and himself were established such warm relations, of affectionate interest on the one side and reverential regard on the other, that Pownoll became a family name among the descendants of the admiral. He himself gave it to his first-born, and it still appears in the present generation. Under him, also, Pellew was brought into direct contact with the American Revolution; for on board the frigate *Blonde,* Pownoll's ship, General Burgoyne embarked in 1775 for Canada, there beginning the undertaking which ended so disastrously for him. It is told that when the distinguished passenger came on board, the yards being manned to receive him with the honors due to his rank, he was startled to see on one yard-arm a midshipman standing on his head. Upon expressing alarm, he was laughingly reassured by the captain, who said that Pellew—for he it was who put this extra touch upon the general's reception—was quite capable of dropping from the yard, passing under the ship's bottom, and coming up on the other side. A few days later the young officer actually did leap from the yard-arm, the ship going fast through the water—not, however, as bravado, but to aid a seaman who had fallen overboard, and whom he succeeded in saving.

Throughout his youth the exuberant vitality of the man delighted in these feats of wanton power. To overturn a boat by press of canvas, as a frolic, is not unexampled among lads of daring; but it is at least unusual, when a hat goes overboard, to follow it into the water, if alone in a boat under sail. This Pellew did, on one occasion, when he was old enough to know better; being at the moment in the open Channel, in a small punt, going from Falmouth to Plymouth. The freak nearly cost him his life; for, though he had lashed the helm down and hove-to the boat, she fell off and gathered way whenever he approached. When at last he laid hold of her rail, after an hour of this fooling, barely strength remained to drag himself on board, where he fell helpless, and waited long before his powers were restored. It is trite to note in such exhibitions of reckless-ness many of the qualities of the ideal seaman, though not so certainly those of the foreordained commander-in-chief. Pellew was a born frigate captain.

At the end of 1775 the Americans were still engaged in the enter-prise against Quebec, the disastrous termination of which is familiarly known. After the fall of General Montgomery in the unsuccessful night assault of December 31, 1775, the American operations were reduced to a land blockade of the town, which was cut off from the sea by ice in the river. A close investment was thus maintained for five months, until the early part of May, 1776, when the place was relieved by the arrival of a small naval force, commanded by Captain Charles Doug-las. Immediately upon its appearance the commanding British general Carleton, attacked the besiegers, who, already prostrated by disease and privation, abandoned their positions and fell back upon Sorel, at the mouth of the river Richelieu, the outlet from Lake Champlain to the St. Lawrence. Here they remained until June, when the enemy, who had received heavy reinforcements, advanced in overpowering numbers. The Americans again retired above the rapids of the Richelieu to St. Johns. Thence there is a clear channel southward; and embarking there, the retreating force without further molestation reached Crown Point, a fortified post a hundred miles distant, at the head of the lake, commanding the narrow stream to which it is reduced in its upper part. Twelve miles above Crown Point is Ticonderoga, the well-known border fortress of the Colonial and Revolutionary wars; and for fifteen or twenty miles farther the stream is navigable for boats of some size, thus affording an easy means of communication in those early days of impassable forests and scanty transport.

Though greatly superior on land, the British had now for a time to stay their pursuit; for the water highway essential to its continuance was controlled by the flotilla under the command of Benedict Arnold, forbidding further advance until it was subdued. The presence of these vessels, which, though few, were as yet unopposed, gained for the Americans, in this hour of extremity, the important respite from June to October, 1776; and then the lateness of the season compelled the postponement of the invasion to the following year. The toil with which this little force had been created, a few months before, was thus amply justified; for delay is ever to the advantage of the defence. In this case it also gave time for a change of commanders on the part of the enemy, from Carleton to Burgoyne, which not improbably had a decisive effect upon the fortunes of the next campaign.

As soon as established at St. Johns, the British took steps to place a naval force upon the lake, an undertaking involving trouble and delay, notwithstanding their greatly superior resources in men and material. Some thirty fighting vessels, suitable to the waters upon which they were to act, were required, and also four hundred bateaux for the transport of the troops. These had either to be built upon the spot, despite the lack of all dockyard facilities, or else to be brought bodily from the St. Lawrence, by road, or through the rapids of the Richelieu, until the deep water at St. Johns was reached. In this hardy, strenuous work, Pellew naturally was conspicuously active; and in its course he gained a particular professional accomplishment which afterwards stood him in good stead.

Several vessels were built upon the shores of the stream; among others, one of one hundred and eighty tons, the *Inflexible*, whose heavier timbers were brought overland to St. Johns. The construction of these craft was superintended by a lieutenant—afterwards Admiral Schank—of scientific knowledge as a ship architect; and through close association with him Pellew's instinctive appreciation of all things nautical received an intelligent guidance, which gave him a quick insight into the probable behavior of a ship from an examination of her build, and enabled him often to suggest a suitable remedy for dangerous faults. During this period of equipment occurred a characteristic incident which has only recently become public through a descendant. "On the day the *Inflexible* was launched, Pellew on the top of the sheers was trying to get in the mainmast. The machinery not being of the best gave way, and down came mainmast, Pellew, and all, into the lake. 'Poor Pellew,' exclaimed Schank, 'he is gone at last!' However, he speedily emerged and was the first man to mount the sheers again. 'Sir,' Admiral Schank used to conclude, 'he was like a squirrel.'" Thirty days after the keel of the *Inflexible* was laid at St. Johns, the vessel herself not only was launched, but had set sail for the southward. She carried eighteen twelve-pounders, nine on a side, and was thus superior in power, not only to any one vessel of the Americans, but to their whole assembled flotilla on Lake Champlain. Except the principal pieces of her hull, the timber of which she was built was hewed in the neighboring forest; and indeed, the whole story of the rapid equipment of this squadron recalls vividly the vigorous preparation of Commander Perry, of the United States navy, in 1813, for his successful attempt to control Lake Erie. The entire British force, land and naval, now moved toward Crown Point. On the 11th of October the American flotilla was discovered, a short distance above Plattsburg and about twenty miles from the foot of the lake, drawn up between Valcour Island and the western shore, which are from one-half to three-fourths of a mile apart. It lay there so snugly that the British, wafted by a northwest wind, had actually passed to the southward without seeing it, and the discovery was purely accidental—a fact which suggests that Arnold, who must have felt the impossibility of a force so inferior as his own contesting, or even long delaying, the enemy's advance by direct opposition, may have entertained some purpose of operating in their rear, and thus causing a diversion which at this late season might effectually arrest their progress. It is true that such a stroke would frightfully imperil his little squadron; but, in circumstances of absolute inferiority, audacity, usually the best policy in war, offers the only chance of success. Mere retreat, however methodical, must end in final destruction. To act towards St. Johns, trusting to dexterity and to local knowledge of the network of islands at the foot of the lake to escape disaster, or at least to protract the issue, offered the best chance; and that the situation thus accepted would not be hopeless was proved by the subsequent temporary evasion of pursuit by the Americans, even in the open and narrow water of the middle lake.

The British moved to attack as soon as the hostile shipping was discovered. Pellew was second officer of the schooner *Carleton*, of twelve guns, the third vessel of the flotilla in point of force. The wind being contrary, and apparently light, the *Carleton* alone of the sailing vessels got into action; and although she was supported by a number of rowing gunboats, whose artillery was heavy, the match was unequal. According to Arnold's own account, he had disposed his gunboats and gondolas "on the west side of Valcour Island, as near together as possible, and in such a form that few vessels can attack us at the same time, and those will be exposed to the fire of the whole fleet." To this Captain Douglas, in his report of the occurrences, adds the suggestive particular that the *Carleton*, by a lucky slant of wind, fetched "nearly into the middle of the rebel half-moon, where she anchored with a spring on her cable." The position was one of honorable distinction, but likewise of great exposure. Her first officer lost an arm; her captain, Lieutenant Dacres, was so severely wounded that he was about to be thrown overboard as dead; and Pellew, thus left without a superior, fought the vessel through the engagement. When signal was at last made to withdraw, the *Carleton* was able to do so only by help of the gunboats, which towed her out of fire. On the other hand, Arnold's flag-ship, the schooner *Royal Savage*, which had fought in advance of her consorts and under canvas, fell to leeward, and came there under the distant fire of the *Inflexible*, by which she was badly crippled. She then was run ashore on the southern point of the island, where she fell momentarily into the hands of the British, who turned her guns on her former friends. Later in the day, it seeming probable that she might be retaken, she was set on fire and burned to the water's edge. Thus abandoned, she sank to the bottom, where her hull rests to this day. During the recent summer of 1901 some gun-carriages have been recovered from her, after lying for a century and a quarter beneath the surface of the lake.

Pellew's personal activity and strength enabled his gallantry to show to particular advantage in this sanguinary contest. When the *Carleton*, in her attempt to withdraw, hung in stays under the island, her decks swept by the bullets of the riflemen on shore, it was he who sprang out on the bowsprit to bear the jib over to windward. When the tow-rope was cut by a shot, it was Pellew again who exposed his person for the safety of the vessel. His two seniors being forced by their wounds to leave the schooner, he succeeded to the command, in which he was afterwards confirmed. In this sharp affair the *Carleton* lost eight killed and six wounded—about half her crew—and had two feet of water in her hold when she anchored out of range.

Towards evening the *Inflexible* succeeded in getting within point-blank range of the American flotilla, "when five broadsides," wrote Douglas, "silenced their whole line;" a sufficient testimony to the superiority of her concentrated battery over the dispersed force of all her numerous petty antagonists. The British then anchored to the southward of Arnold's little force; but that active and enterprising officer succeeded in stealing during the night between the enemy and the western shore, and retired towards Crown Point. The chase to windward continued during the next day, but a favorable shift of wind, to the north, reached the British first, and enabled them to close. Arnold again behaved with the extraordinary bravery and admirable conduct which distinguished him in battle. Sending on the bulk of the squadron, he took the rear with two galleys, covering the retreat. Fighting like a lion, he opposed the enemy's advance long enough to secure the escape of six of his vessels; and then, seeing his one consort forced to strike, he ran his own galley ashore and set her on fire. "Arnold," says the naval historian Cooper, "covered himself with glory, and his example seems to have been nobly followed by most of his officers and men. The manner in which the Congress was fought until she had covered the retreat of the galleys, and the stubborn resolution with which she was defended until destroyed, converted the disasters of this part of the day into a species of triumph." "The Americans," says a contemporary British writer, "chiefly gloried in the dangerous attention paid by Arnold to a nice point of honor, in keeping his flag flying, and not quitting his galley till she was in flames, lest the enemy should have boarded and struck it."

Pellew received like recognition, not, perhaps, from the popular voice, but from his official superiors. Douglas, the senior naval officer at Quebec, who was made a baronet in reward of these operations, Lord Howe at New York, and the First Lord of the Admiralty in England, all sent him personal letters of commendation; and the two latter promised him promotion as soon as he came within their respective jurisdictions. His continuance at the front of operations during this and the following year therefore postponed his deserved advancement to a lieutenancy, by retaining him from the "jurisdiction" of those able to bestow it.

The two gallant enemies were soon again brought together in an incident which came near to change the career of one of them, and, in so doing, to modify seriously the fortunes of many others. Arnold having one day pulled out on the open lake, in his venturesome manner, Pellew gave chase in another boat. The Americans being hard pressed and capture probable, Arnold unbuckled his stock and himself took an oar. So nearly caught was he, that he had to escape into the bushes, leaving behind him stock and buckle; and these, as late as sixty years after, remained in the possession of Pellew's brother. Had he thus been deprived of the opportunity that Saratoga gave him the next year, Arnold's name might now be known to us only as that of the brave officer who kept his country's flag flying till his vessel was in flames.

On the 14th of October Carleton landed at Crown Point, which the Americans had abandoned; but the lateness of the season deterred him from advancing against Ticonderoga, and he soon afterwards returned to Canada. The full import of this halt is too easily overlooked, with consequent failure to appreciate the momentous influence exerted upon the course of the Revolutionary War by this naval campaign, in which Pellew bore so conspicuous a part. It has never been understood in America, where the smallness of the immediate scale has withdrawn attention from the greatness of the ultimate issue, in gaining time for the preparations which resulted in the admittedly decisive victories about Saratoga. "If we could have begun our expedition four weeks earlier," wrote a German general there present, "I am satisfied everything would have been ended this year [1776]; were our whole army here, it would be an easy matter to drive the enemy from their entrenchments at Ticonderoga." The delay, not of four weeks only, but of the whole summer, was obtained by the naval force organized upon Champlain by Arnold and his superior, General Schuyler. The following year the invasion was resumed, under General Burgoyne. Pellew accompanied him with a body of seamen, taking part in all the operations down to the final surrender. Burgoyne, indeed, afterwards chaffed him with being the cause of the disaster, by rebuilding the bridge which enabled the army to cross from the east bank of the Hudson to the west.

Returning to England in the early part of 1778, Pellew was made lieutenant, and in 1780 we find him again serving under Captain Pownoll, as first lieutenant of the *Apollo* frigate. On the 15th of June, in the same year, the *Apollo* met the French frigate *Stanislas*. A severe action followed, and at the end of an hour Pownoll was shot through the body. As his young friend raised him from the deck, he had barely time to say, "Pellew, I know you won't give his Majesty's ship away," and immediately expired. The engagement lasted an hour longer, when the enemy, which had all the time been standing in for the Belgian coast, took the ground, the most of her spars, already wounded, going overboard with the shock. The *Apollo* had hauled off a few moments before, finding that she had less than five feet of water under her keel.

Though unable again to attack the *Stanislas*, which claimed the protection of the neutral flag, the result was substantially a victory; but to Pellew's grief for the death of a tried friend was added the material loss of a powerful patron. Happily, however, his reputation was known to the head of the Admiralty, who not only promoted him for this action, but also gave him a ship, though a poor one. After a succession of small commands, he was fortunate enough again to distinguish himself,—driving ashore and destroying several French privateers, under circumstances of such danger and difficulty as to win him his next grade, post-captain. This step, which, so far as selection went, fixed his position in the navy, he received on the 25th of May, 1782.

The ten years of peace that shortly followed were passed by many officers in retirement, which we have seen was contentedly accepted by his distinguished contemporary, Saumarez; but Pellew was a seaman to the marrow, and constantly sought employment afloat. When out of occupation, he for a while tried farming, the Utopian employment that most often beguiles the imagination of the inbred seaman in occasional weariness of salt water; but, as his biographer justly remarks, his mind, which allowed him to be happy only when active, could ill accommodate itself to pursuits that almost forbade exertion. "To have an object in view, yet to be unable to advance it by any exertions of his own, was to him a source of constant irritation. He was wearied with the imperceptible growth of his crops, and complained that he made his eyes ache by watching their daily progress."

His assiduous applications, however, were not wholly unavailing to obtain him the professional employments usually so hard to get in times of peace. For five of the ten years, 1783–1793, he commanded frigates, chiefly on the Newfoundland station; and in them, though now turning thirty, he displayed the superabundant vitality and restless activity that had characterized his early youth. "Whenever there was exertion required aloft," wrote a midshipman who served with him at this period, "to preserve a sail or a mast, the captain was foremost in the work, apparently as a mere matter of amusement, and there was not a man in the ship that could equal him in personal activity. He appeared to play among the elements in the hardest storms. I remember once, in close-reefing the main topsail, the captain had given his orders from the quarter-deck and sent us aloft. On gaining the topsail yard, the most active and daring of our party hesitated to go upon it, as the sail was flapping violently, making it a service of great danger; but a voice was heard from the extreme end of the yard, calling upon us to exert ourselves to save the sail, which would otherwise beat to pieces. A man said, 'Why, that's the captain! How the did he get there?' He had followed us up, and, clambering over the backs of the sailors, had reached the topmast head, above the yard, and thence descended by the lift,"—a feat unfortunately not easy to be explained to landsmen, but which will be allowed by seamen to demand great hardihood and address.

All this was the simple overflow of an animal energy not to be repressed, the exulting prowess of a giant delighting to run his course. It found expression also in joyous practical jests, like those of a big boy, which at times had ludicrous consequences. On one occasion of state ceremony, the king's birthday, Pellew had dressed in full uniform to attend a dinner on shore. The weather was hot, and the crew had been permitted an hour's swimming around the ship. While his boat was being manned, the captain stood by the frigate's rail watching the bathers, and near by him was one of the ship's boys. "I too shall have a good swim soon," called the latter to a comrade in the water. "The sooner, the better," said Pellew, coming behind him and tipping him overboard. No sooner had the lad risen to the surface from his plunge than it was plain that he could not swim; so in after him went the practical joker, with all his toggery. "If ever the captain was frightened," writes the officer just quoted, "it was then."

But along with all this physical exuberance and needless assumption of many of the duties of a foremast hand, Pellew possessed to a very remarkable extent that delicate art of seamanship which consists in so handling a ship as to make her do just what you want, and to put her just where she should be; making her, to use a common sea expression, do everything but talk. This is a faculty probably inborn, like most others that reach any great degree of perfection, and, while a very desirable gift, it is by no means indispensable to the highest order of naval excellence. Nelson did not at all equal Pellew in this respect, as is indicated by an amusing story transmitted by a Colonel Stewart, who served on board the great admiral's flag-ship during the expedition against Copenhagen: "His lordship was rather too apt to interfere in the working of the ship, and not always with the best judgment or success. The wind, when off Dungeness, was scanty, and the ship was to be put about. Lord Nelson would give the orders, and caused her to miss stays. Upon this he said, rather peevishly, to the officer of the watch, 'Well, now see what we have done. Well, sir, what mean you to do now?' The officer saying, with hesitation, 'I don't exactly know, my lord. I fear she won't do,' Lord Nelson turned sharply to the cabin, and replied, 'Well, I am sure if you do not know what to do with her, no more do I, either.' He went in, leaving the officer to work the ship as he liked." Yet Nelson understood perfectly what ships could do, and what they could not; no one could better handle or take care of a fleet, or estimate the possibility of performing a given manoeuvre; and long before he was called to high command he was distinguished for a knowledge of naval tactics to which few, if any other, of his time attained. He was a great general officer; and whether he had the knack of himself making a ship go through all her paces without a fault mattered as little as whether he was a crack shot with a gun.

A ship is certainly the most beautiful and most graceful of machines; a machine, too, so varied in its movements and so instinct with life that the seaman affectionately transfers to her credit his own virtues in handling her. Pellew's capacity in this part of his profession was so remarkable that it is somewhat singular to find him, in his first frigate action, compelled to discard manoeuvring, and to rely for victory upon sheer pluck and luck. When war with the French republic began in 1793, his high reputation immediately insured him command of a frigate, the *Nymphe*. The strength of England as a naval power lay largely in the great reserve of able seamen manning her merchant ships; but as these were scattered in all quarters of the world, great embarrassment was commonly felt at the outbreak of a war, and especially when it came with the unexpected rapidity of the revolutionary fury. As the object of first importance was to get the fleets of ships-of-the-line to sea, Pellew had to depend chiefly upon his own indefatigable exertions to procure a crew for his vessel. Seamen being hard to find, he had on board a disproportionate number of landsmen when the *Nymphe*, on the 19th of June, 1793, encountered the French vessel *Cleopatre*, of force slightly inferior, except in men, but not sufficiently so to deny the victor the claim of an even fight.

A peculiar incident preceding the action has interest, as showing the strong preoccupation of men's minds at the opening of war, before meetings with the enemy have lost novelty. Pellew's younger brother, Israel, a commander in the navy, being otherwise unemployed, had come out with him for the cruise. The *Cleopatre* having been first seen in the early morning, Edward would not have him called till just as the *Nymphe* was closing. As he came on deck, the brother said affectionately, "Israel, you have no business here. We are too many eggs from one nest. I am sorry I brought you from your wife." But the other was unheeding, his eyes fixed upon the stranger. "That's the very frigate," he cried, "that I've been dreaming of all night! I dreamt that we shot away her wheel." And, hastening to the after-gun, he made the French ship's wheel the object of an unremitting fire.

By the way the enemy was handled it was evident that she was well manned and ably commanded. She had, in fact, been in commission for over a year. Great as was his own skill, Pellew could not venture upon manoeuvres with a green crew, untrained save at the guns, and only filled the night before by pressing from a merchant vessel. He therefore determined upon a simple artillery duel. The Frenchman waited under short canvas, while the *Nymphe*, with greater way, drew slowly up on his starboard, or right-hand side; both ships running nearly before the wind, but having it a little on the left side. Each captain stood uncovered, and as the bows of the *Nymphe* doubled upon the stern of the *Cleopatre*, within three hundred feet, a French sailor was seen to run aloft and fasten a red cap of liberty to the mainmast head. The eyes of the British seamen were fastened upon their commander, awaiting the gesture which he had set, instead of word of mouth, for opening fire. At quarter-past six he gave it, raising his cap to his head. A furious cannonade at once began, and, the *Nymphe* shortening sail as soon as fairly abreast her antagonist, the two frigates continued on parallel lines, maintaining their relative positions as though at anchor, and rolling easily in the soft summer sea under the recoil of their guns. So nearly matched were the gunners that the conflict, unusually deadly though it was, might have lasted long, but at a little before seven Israel Pellew's dream was fulfilled. The Frenchman's wheel was shot away, and, the mizzenmast going overboard at the same time, the *Cleopatre* yielded to the impulse of her forward sails, turned sharp round to the right, and ran perpendicularly into the *Nymphe*. The British boarded her, fixed in this disadvantageous position, fought their way aft, and, although the French crew was numerically superior, in ten minutes hauled down the colors. In this brief hour they had lost twenty-three killed and twenty-seven wounded, the enemy sixty-three killed and wounded, out of ships' companies numbering respectively two hundred and forty and three hundred and twenty.

This was the first decisive frigate action of the War of the French Revolution, and in consequence great was the enthusiasm aroused. Lord Howe wrote to Pellew, "The manner in which you have taken the enemy's ship will set an example for the war." In truth, however, while admitting the soundness of Pellew's judgment in adopting the course he did, the actual demand upon his personal skill was less, and in so far the credit due therefore less, than in the second successful frigate action, in the following October, in which Sir James Saumarez commanded. Not only was the French vessel's superiority in force more marked in the latter instance, but Saumarez's ship there met with an accident similar in character to that which befell the *Cleopatre*, from the consequences of which she was extricated by his masterly seamanship. Still, it may with fairness be argued that, as the one action from its attendant circumstances evidenced the individual skill of the commander, so the other testified to the antecedent preparation and efficiency of the crew, which are always to be attributed to the care of the captain, especially under the conditions of Pellew's enlistments. Both captains fully deserved the reward of knighthood bestowed upon their success. Israel Pellew was promoted to post-captain.

During the first three years of this war British commerce in the neighborhood of the Channel suffered most severely from French cruisers. The latter resumed the methods of Jean Bart and other celebrated privateers of the days of Louis XIV; the essence of which was to prey upon the enemy's commerce, not by single vessels, but by small squadrons of from five to seven. Cruisers so combined, acting in mutual support, were far more efficient than the same number acting separately. Spreading like a fan, they commanded a wider expanse than a ship alone; if danger arose, they concentrated for mutual support; did opportunity offer, the work was cut out and distributed, thus insuring by co-operation more thorough results. At the suggestion of Sir Edward Pellew, the British Admiralty determined to oppose to these organized depredators a similar system. Groups of crack frigates were constituted, and sent to cruise within the limits of the Channel Fleet, but independent of its admiral. In these Pellew served for the next five years, much of the time as squadron commander; to him a period of incessant, untiring activity, and illustrated by many brilliant and exciting incidents, for which the limits of this sketch afford no space.

There are, however, two episodes in which he was so distinctly the central figure that they demand at least a brief narration. In January, 1796, while his ship was repairing, a large East Indiaman, the *Dutton*, carrying some six hundred troops and passengers, was by a series of mishaps driven ashore on the beach of Plymouth, then an unprotected sound. As she struck, all her masts went overboard, and she lay broadside to the waves, pounding heavily as they broke over her. Pellew was at this moment driving to a dinner with his wife. Seeing crowds running from various directions towards the same quarter, he asked the reason. Upon learning it, he left his carriage and hurried to the scene. When he arrived, he recognized, by the confusion on board, by the way the ship was laboring, by the poverty of the means that had been contrived for landing the imperilled souls—only a single hawser having been run to the shore—that the loss of nearly all on board was imminent. Night, too, was falling, as well as the destruction of the vessel impending. After vainly offering rewards to the hardy boatmen standing by, if they would board the wreck with a message from him, he said, "Then I must go myself." Though then close to forty years of age, his immense personal strength and activity enabled him, though sorely bruised thereby, to be hauled on board through the breakers by the hawser, which alternately slacked and then tightened with a jerk as the doomed ship rolled to and fro in the seas. Once on board, he assumed command, the want of which, through the absence of the proper captain, had until then hampered and well-nigh paralyzed all effectual effort. When his well-known name was spoken, three hearty cheers arose from the troops on board, echoed by the thousands of spectators on shore; and the hope that revived with the presence of a born leader of men showed itself at once in the renewed activity and intelligent direction of effort, on the decks and on the beach. The degree of the danger can be estimated from the fact that boats from the ships of war in port, his own included, tried in vain to approach and had to run for safety to the inner harbor. With sword drawn—for many of the soldiers were drunk and riotous—Pellew maintained order, guided with a seaman's readiness the preparations for landing, and saw the women, the children—one child but three weeks old—the sick, landed first, then the soldiers, lastly the seamen. When he himself was transferred to the beach by the same means that his skill had contrived for others, but three persons remained on board, officers of the ship, who eased him on shore. The injuries he had received in his perilous passage out, and which confined him to his bed for a week, forbade his being last. To the end of his life, this saving of the crew of the *Dutton* was the action in which he took most pride.

The year that opened with this magnificent act of self-devotion saw Pellew, at its close, bearing a seaman's part in the most serious crisis that befell his country during the wars of the French Revolution. The end of 1796 and the earlier months of 1797 marked the nadir of Great Britain's military fortunes. The successes of Bonaparte's Italian campaign were then culminating; Austria was on the point of making peace with France; England was about to find herself alone, and the discontent of the seamen of the navy, long smouldering, was soon to break out into the famous and threatening mutinies of the Channel Fleet and of the Nore. At the same time France, relieved on her eastern frontiers, felt able to devote seventeen ships-of-the-line and eighteen thousand troops to the invasion of Ireland.

Pellew, with two frigates besides his own, was stationed off the mouth of Brest harbor to watch the enemy's movements; the main British fleet being some fifty miles to seaward. To this emergency he brought not only the intrepidity of a great seaman and the ardor of an anxious patriot, but likewise the intense though narrow Protestant feeling transmitted from a past, then not so remote, when Romanism and enmity to England were almost synonymous. "How would you like," said he to an officer who shared Pitt's liberal tendencies, "to see Roman Catholic chaplains on board our ships?" and to the end of his life he opposed the political enfranchisement of persons of that creed.

The French expedition against Ireland sailed from Brest on the 16th of December, 1796. Having sent off successively each of his consorts with information for the fleet, Pellew remained with his own ship alone, the *Indefatigable,* at the moment of the final start. There are two principal channels by which Brest can be left, one leading to the south, the other due west. The French admiral had at first intended to use the former; but, the wind showing signs of an unfavorable shift, he endeavored to change the orders just as night was falling. The weather being hazy, his signals were understood by but few of the forty-odd vessels composing the force. Eight or ten joined him; the remainder followed the original instructions and went out by the south. Pellew attached himself to the admiral's division, kept along with it just out of gunshot, and by making false signals, burning blue lights and sending up rockets, introduced into the attempts to convey the wishes of the commander-in-chief such confusion as rendered them utterly futile. Having satisfied himself as to the general direction taken by the enemy, he left them, and made all sail for Falmouth, where he arrived on the 20th.

The general fortunes of the expedition do not belong to the present story. Suffice it to say that the greater part reached Ireland safely, but through stress of weather was unable to land the troops, and went back to France by detachments, in January, 1797. It is during this process of return that Sir Edward Pellew again appears, in perhaps the most dramatic incident of his stirring career.

On the afternoon of January 13th, being then in company with the frigate *Amazon,* and about one hundred and twenty miles west of Brest, a French ship-of-the-line was discovered. The stranger, named the *Droits de l'Homme,* was returning from Ireland, and heading east. The frigates steered courses converging towards hers, seeking to cut her off from the land. The weather was thick and gloomy, with a strong west wind fast rising to a gale. At half-past four, as night was falling, the French ship carried away her fore and main topmasts in a heavy squall; and an hour later the *Indefatigable,* now under close reefs, passed across her stern, pouring in a broadside from so near that the French flag floated across her poop, where it was seized and torn away by some of the British seamen. The enemy, having on board nearly a thousand soldiers besides her crew, replied with rapid volleys of musketry, and, as the frigate passed ahead, sheered impetuously towards her, attempting to board, and in her turn grazing the stern of the *Indefatigable.* In another hour the *Amazon* drew up, and then the British vessels took their positions, one on either bow of the *Droits de l'Homme,* whence, by movements of the helm, they alternately raked her. The labor of the gunners, however, was arduous, due to the deep rolling of the ships, on board which, also, the seas poured in volumes through the gun-ports. On the main decks the men fought up to their middles in water, the heavy cannon broke away from the breechings, or ropes used to control them, and even iron bolts tore out from the ships' sides under the severe recoil of the guns. Thus through the long winter night the three ships rushed headlong before the gale towards the French coast, intent on mutual destruction; the constant storm of shot, though flying wild under the violent motions of the vessels, tearing through spars and rigging, and crippling them in much that was essential to their safety.

At four o'clock in the morning of the 14th, long before daybreak, land was sighted right ahead. The *Indefatigable* hauled at once to the southward, the *Amazon* to the northward; the enemy alone, seemingly unconscious of the danger, kept on, and as she passed Pellew's ship fired a broadside which severely wounded all the masts. The situation of the combatants was well-nigh desperate. They had reached the coast of France at a point where it forms a deep recess, called Audierne Bay, from either side of which project capes that must be cleared in order to gain once more the open sea. One only of the three escaped. The *Droits de l'Homme,* unmanageable for want of sail power, tried to anchor, but drove, and struck on a shoal some distance from the beach. Of sixteen hundred souls on board when the battle began, over one hundred had been killed; and of those who survived the fight three hundred perished in the wreck. The *Amazon,* likewise crippled, though not so badly, had gone ashore to the northward only ten minutes after she ceased firing. Of her people, but six were drowned. The *Indefatigable,* beating back and forth against the gale before the scene of the French disaster, upon which her crew gazed with the solemn feeling that such might soon be their own fate, succeeded at last in clearing the southern cape. At eleven o'clock, nearly twenty-four hours after first meeting the foe, and with six feet of water in her hold, she passed only three-quarters of a mile outside of the Penmarcks, a rocky promontory thirty miles south of Brest.

This remarkable encounter is said to have suggested to Marryat the vivid sea picture with which "The King's Own" ends. Pellew's unusual personal endurance was signally illustrated on the same day, very shortly after the safety of the ship from wreck was assured. Her principal sails had been so torn by shot as to require immediate renewing, and this had scarcely been done when two vessels were sighted, one of which was for the moment supposed to be the *Amazon*, whose fate was yet unknown. Pellew gave orders to chase, but his officers represented to him that, whatever he himself was capable of, the ship's company was too exhausted for present further exertion; and that, besides, the ammunition was very short, almost the last filled cartridge having been expended. Under these circumstances he was compelled to desist.

The interest of Pellew's career centres mainly in his command of frigates. This independent but yet restricted sphere afforded the fullest scope for a conspicuous display of those splendid qualities—fearlessness, enterprise, sound judgment, instant decision, and superb seamanship—which he so eminently possessed. He was, above all, the frigate captain. "Nothing like hesitation was ever seen in him. His first order was always his last; and he often declared of himself that he never had a second thought worth sixpence." In 1799, by a new Admiralty rule, he was transferred to the *Impetueux*, a ship-of-the-line, and thenceforth served in that class of vessel until his promotion to admiral.

As a general officer, Pellew had no opportunity to show whether he possessed ability of the highest order. For five years he held the command in India; and soon after Collingwood's death he was, in 1811, appointed commander-in-chief in the Mediterranean. On both stations he evinced that faculty for careful organization, systematic preparation, and sagacious distribution of force which carries success up to the point which administrative capacity can reach. His ability in planning, while yet a subordinate in command of squadrons, had been recognized by St. Vincent during his management of the Brest blockade. "The disposition made by Sir Edward Pellew for the descent on a certain point is the most masterly I have ever seen. . . . Although the naval command in Quiberon may appear too important for a captain, I shall not divest him of it, unless I am ordered to do so; feeling a thorough conviction that no man in His Majesty's Navy, be his rank ever so high, will fill it so well." At the time this was written, June, 1800, he had seven ships-of-the-line under his orders. After the Peace of Amiens, when war again began in 1803, he commanded a similar division watching the Spanish port of Ferrol, in which, although formally neutral, a French division lay at anchor; and in discharge of this duty, both as a seaman and an administrator, he again justified the eulogium of the old Earl, now at the head of the navy as First Lord.

In 1804 he was promoted Rear-Admiral, and soon afterwards assigned to the East India Station, which he held from 1805 to 1809. Here no naval actions on the great scale were to be fought, but under his systematic organization of convoys and cruisers for the protection of commerce the insurance premium—the war risk—on the most exposed routes fell markedly—for the port of Bombay fifty per cent less than at any former period of hostilities; while the losses by capture, when the merchants observed his instructions, amounted to but one per cent on the property insured, which was less than those caused by the dangers of the sea, and considerably less, also, than the average war losses in other parts of the world. All this shows great ability, carefully utilized in diligent preparation and efficient precaution; and the same characteristics are to be observed in his administration of the Mediterranean command, of wider scope and more purely military importance. Nevertheless, it gives no sure proof of the particular genius of a great captain. Whether, having forged his weapon, Pellew could also wield it; whether, having carefully sowed, he could also reap the harvest by large combinations on the battle-field, must remain uncertain, at least until probable demonstration of his conceptions is drawn from his papers. Nothing is as yet adduced to warrant positive inference.

Pellew's Mediterranean command coincided in time with the period of Napoleon's falling fortunes. After Trafalgar, the Emperor decided to increase his navy largely, but to keep it in port instead of at sea, forcing Great Britain also to maintain huge fleets, the expense of which, concurring with the commercial embarrassments that he sought to bring upon her, might exhaust her power to continue the war. In consequence of this policy, British military achievement on the grand scale was confined to the army in the Spanish peninsula; and in the bestowal of rewards, after Napoleon's first abdication, but one peerage was given to the navy. The great claims of Sir James Saumarez, who was the senior of the two, were disregarded on the ground that his flag was not flying at the moment, and Pellew was created Baron Exmouth.

During the process of settlement which succeeded the final fall of Napoleon at Waterloo, Lord Exmouth remained in the Mediterranean. In the early part of 1816 he was ordered to visit with his fleet the Barbary ports, and to compel the unconditional release of all slaves who were natives of the Ionian Islands; they having become subjects of Great Britain by the terms of the peace. For many years, while the powers of Europe were engrossed in the tremendous strife of the French Revolution, these piratical states, under pretence of regular hostilities, had preyed upon the coasts as well as upon the commerce of the weak Mediterranean countries, and captives taken by them were kept in bitter slavery. Nelson in his correspondence, in 1796, mentions a curious incident which sufficiently characterizes the general motives and policy of these barbarian Courts. He asked an Algerine official visiting his ship, why the Dey would not make peace with Genoa and Naples, for they would pay well for immunity, as the United States also at that time did. The reply was, "If we make peace with every one, what is the Dey to do with his ships?" In his later experience with the Mediterranean the great admiral realized yet more forcibly the crying shame of Great Britain's acquiescence. "My blood boils that I cannot chastise these pirates. They could not show themselves in this sea did not our country permit. Never let us talk of the cruelty of the African slave trade, while we permit such a horrid war." The United States alone, although then among the least of naval powers, had taken arms before 1805 to repress outrages that were the common reproach of all civilized nations—a measure the success of which went far to establish the character of her navy and prepare it for 1812. Lord Exmouth was also directed to demand peace for Sardinia, as well as for any other state that should authorize him to act for it. Only Naples availed itself of this opportunity.

As far as his instructions went, his mission was successful, and, by a happy accident, he was able at Tunis and Tripoli to extort further from the rulers a promise that thereafter captives should be treated as in civilized countries; in other words, that they should no longer be reduced to slavery. Algiers refused this concession; and the admiral could not take steps to enforce it, because beyond his commission. The Dey, however, undertook to consult the Porte; and the fleet, with a few exceptions, returned to England, where it arrived towards the end of June.

Meanwhile British public feeling had become aroused; for men were saying that the outrages of the past had been rather welcome to the commercial selfishness of the country. The well-protected traders of Great Britain, shielded by her omnipotent navy, had profited by crimes which drove their weaker rivals from the sea. Just then news came that at the port of Bona, on the Algiers coast, where there was under the British flag an establishment for carrying on the coral fishery, a large number of the fishermen, mostly Italians, had been wantonly slaughtered by a band of Turkish troops. To insist, arms in hand, upon reparation for such an outrage, and upon guarantees for the future, would doubtless be condemned by some of our recent lights; but such was not then the temper of Great Britain. The government determined at once to send a fleet to the spot, and Lord Exmouth was chosen for the command, with such a force as he himself should designate. The gist of his instructions was to demand the release, without ransom, of *all* Christian slaves, and a solemn declaration from the Dey that, in future wars, prisoners should receive the usage accorded them by European states. Great Britain thus made herself, as befitted the obligation imposed by her supreme maritime power, the avenger of all those oppressed by these scourges of the sea. The times of the barbarians were fulfilled.

During a long career of successful piracy, the port of Algiers had accumulated an extensive and powerful system of defenses. These had doubtless suffered in condition from the nonchalant fatalism of Turkish rule, encouraged by a long period of impunity; but they constituted still, and under all the shortcomings of the defenders, a most imposing menace to an attacking fleet. To convey a precise impression of them by detailed verbal description would be difficult, and the attempt probably confusing. It may be said, in brief, that the town faces easterly, rising abruptly up a steep hill; that from its front there then projected a pier, nearly a thousand feet long, at whose end was a circular fort, carrying seventy guns in three tiers; from that point a mole extended at right angles to the southward—parallel, that is, in a general sense, to the town front, but curving inward through the southern half of its length, so as better to embrace and shelter the vessels inside. This mole was somewhat over a thousand feet in length, and had throughout two tiers of guns, linked at their northern extremity to the circular fort at the pier end. These principal works were flanked and covered, at either end and on the hillside, by others which it is unnecessary to particularize. The total number of guns bearing seaward numbered near three hundred, of very respectable size for that day. The basin formed by the pier and the mole constituted the port proper, and in it, at the time of the attack, was collected the entire Algerine navy, nine frigates and corvettes and thirty-seven gunboats, the paltry force that had so long terrorized the Mediterranean.

In prevision of his present enterprise, Lord Exmouth before leaving the Mediterranean had despatched a light cruiser to Algiers, on a casual visit similar to those continually made by ships of war to foreign ports. Her commander, Captain Charles Warde, received from him very precise and most secret instructions to examine closely into the defences and soundings; to do which it was necessary not only to observe every precaution of seeming indifference—even to the extent of appearing engrossed with social duties—but also to conduct under this cover measurements and observations of at least approximate correctness. This duty was performed with singular diligence and success, with the double result of revealing the hopeless inaccuracy of existing charts and of placing in Exmouth's hands a working plan of the ground, perfectly trustworthy for his tactical dispositions.

As before remarked, in the sketch of Lord St. Vincent, the defence and attack of seaports, involving as they do both occupation of permanent positions and the action of mobile bodies, are tactical questions. They differ much, though not radically, from operations in the open sea, or in the field, where positions may be taken incidentally, but where the movements of mobile bodies are the principal factor. In this way, though without using the word tactical, Exmouth treated the problem before him. Furnished, thanks to his own foresight and Warde's efficiency, with reliable information concerning the preparations of the enemy, he calculated the dispositions necessary to meet them and to crush their fire. Having assigned to the hostile works, severally and collectively, the force needed to overbear them, and having arranged the anchoring positions for the vessels of his command with reference to the especial task of each, as well as for mutual support, he had substantially his plan of battle, afterwards communicated to the fleet before going into action; and the same data afforded the foundation for his statement to the Government of the number and character of ships needed for success.

To the surprise of the Admiralty, Lord Exmouth asked for but five ships-of-the-line, five frigates, and five smaller vessels, to which were added four mortar boats to play upon the town and arsenal. When met with expressions of doubt, he replied, "I am satisfied, and take the responsibility entirely upon myself." To satisfy the hesitancy of the Government, he left with the Secretary to the Admiralty a written statement that his every requirement had been fulfilled, and that to him alone, therefore, would failure from deficient power be attributable. On the eve of departure he said to his brother Israel, "If they open fire when the ships are coming up, and cripple them in their masts, the difficulty and loss will be greater; but if they allow us to take our stations, I am sure of them, for I know that nothing can resist a line-of-battle ship's fire." He trusted to the extreme care of his preparations, which neglected no particular of equipment or organization, elaborating every detail of training and discipline, and providing, by the most diligent foresight and minute instruction, that each officer concerned should know exactly what was expected of him. In short, it was to perfection of quality, and not to an unwieldy bulk of superfluous quantity, that Exmouth confided his fortunes in this last hazard.

The fleet sailed from England on the 28th of July, 1816, was joined at Gibraltar by a Dutch squadron of five frigates, whose commander asked to share the coming contest, and on the 26th of August was off the north point of Algiers Bay, some twenty miles from the town. At daybreak the next morning, the weather being almost calm, a flag of truce was sent in, bearing the British demands. During its absence a breeze from the sea sprang up, and the fleet stood in to a mile from the works, where it stopped to await the reply. At two p.m. the boat was seen returning, with the signal that no answer had been given. The flag-ship queried, "Are you ready?" Each ship at once replied, "Yes;" and all filling away together stood down to the attack, the admiral leading.

The Algerine batteries were fully manned; the mole, moreover, was crowded with troops. With singular temerity, they fired no gun as the ships came on, thus relieving the most anxious of Exmouth's preoccupations concerning the difficulties before him; fearing, seemingly, that, if otherwise received, the prey might turn and escape. The British, on their side, observed the utmost silence; not a gun, not a cheer, marred the solemn impression of the approach. The flag-ship, *Queen Charlotte* piloted by an officer who had served continuously with Exmouth since 1793, anchored by the stern across the mole head, at a distance of fifty yards, her starboard batteries pointing to sweep it from end to end. Still no sound of battle, as she proceeded to lash her bows to those of an

Algerine brig lying just within the mole. This done, her crew gave three cheers, as well they might. Then the stolid, unaccountable apathy of the barbarians ceased, and three guns in quick succession were fired from the eastern battery. Stirred by a movement of compassion, Lord Exmouth, from the flagship's poop, seeing the Moorish soldiery clustered thick upon the parapets to watch the ships, waved to them with his hand to get down. At the first hostile gun he gave the order "Stand by!" at the second, "Fire!" and simultaneously with the third the *Queen Charlotte's* broadside rang out, and the battle began.

The other vessels of the squadron were not all as successful as the flag-ship in taking the exact position assigned, and the admiral's plan thereby suffered some of that derangement to which every undertaking, especially military and naval, is liable. This, however, produced no effect upon the general result, except by increasing somewhat the lists of killed and wounded, through loss of advantageous offensive position, with consequent defect in mutual support. But the first broadside is proverbially half the battle. It was a saying of Collingwood to his crew, in a three-decker like the *Queen Charlotte*, that if they could deliver three effective fires in the first five minutes no vessel could resist them; and this was yet more certain when opposed to the semi-discipline of adversaries such as the Algerine pirates. Exmouth's general design was to concentrate his heavy ships at the southern end of the mole, whence the curve in the line of batteries would enable them to enfilade or take in reverse the works at the northern extremity. Here were to be the two three-deckers, with a seventy-four between them, all three in close order, stem to stern. The two-decker, however, anchored some seven hundred feet astern of the *Queen Charlotte*, the intervening space being left empty until filled by a thirty-six-gun frigate, upon whose captain St. Vincent passed the eulogium, "He seems to have felt Lord Nelson's eye upon him." The two remaining seventy-fours placed themselves successively close astern of the first, which was in accord with the original purpose, while the other three-decker took the right flank of the line, and somewhat too far out; in which exposed and unintended position, beyond the extreme north point contemplated for the British order, she underwent a very heavy loss.

In general summary, therefore, it may be said that the broadsides of the ships-of-the-line were opposed from end to end to the heavy central batteries on the mole, while the lighter vessels engaged the flanking works on the shore to the southward, thus diverting the fire which would have harassed the chief assailants—a service in which the Dutch squadron, composed entirely of frigates, rendered important assistance. The bomb vessels from the rear threw their shells over the fighting ships into the town and arsenal, and in the admiral's report are credited with firing all the shipping in the harbor, except one frigate, creating a conflagration which spread over the arsenal and storehouses. Soon after the contest opened, the thirty-seven Algerine gunboats, crowded with troops, were seen advancing under cover of the smoke to board the flag-ship. The attempt, rash to insanity, met the fate it should have expected; thirty-three were sent to the bottom by the guns of the *Leander*, stationed ahead of the *Queen Charlotte*, and commanding the entrance to the port. An hour later, Lord Exmouth determined to set fire to the remaining frigate. The service was performed by an officer and boat's crew, with a steadiness which elicited from him such admiration that, on the return of the party, he stopped the working of the ship's upper battery to give them three cheers. As the hostile vessel burned, she drifted so near the *Queen Charlotte* as nearly to involve her in the same fate.

From three to ten p.m. the battle lasted, steady disciplined valor contending with a courage in no way inferior, absolutely insensible to danger, but devoid of that coherent, skilful direction which is to courage what the brain and eye are to the heart. "I never," wrote Exmouth to his brother, "saw any set of men more obstinate at their guns, and it was superior fire only that could keep them back. To be sure, nothing could stand before the *Queen Charlottes* broadside. Everything fell before it, and the Swedish consul assures me we killed above five hundred at the very first fire, from the crowded way in which the troops were drawn up, four deep above the gunboats, which were also full of men. It was a glorious sight," he continues, "to see the *Charlotte* take her anchorage, and to see her flag towering on high, when she appeared to be in the flames of the mole itself; and never was a ship nearer burnt; it almost scorched me off the poop. We were obliged to haul in the ensign, or it would have caught fire." He was himself struck thrice, though not seriously injured. A cannon-ball carried away the skirts of his coat, and one glass of the spectacles in his pocket was broken, and the frame bulged, by a shot.

At ten p.m., the ammunition of the fleet running short, and its work being substantially accomplished, the ships began to haul off. The sea defences and a great part of the town were in ruins. "To be again effective," wrote Exmouth, "the defences must be rebuilt from the foundation." The flanking batteries and the hill forts continued to annoy the vessels as they retired, but the spirit of the Dey was broken. Towards eleven a light air from the land sprang up, which freshened into a violent and prolonged thunderstorm, lasting for three hours; and the flashes of heaven's artillery combined with the glare of the burning town to illuminate the withdrawal of the ships.

The following morning the Dey signified his submission, and on the 30th of August Lord Exmouth made known to the fleet that all the terms of Great Britain had been yielded; that Christian slavery was forever abolished, and that by noon of the following day all slaves then in Algiers would be delivered to his flag. This was accordingly done, the whole number amounting to 1642; which, with those previously released at Tunis and Tripoli, raised to 3003 the human beings whom Exmouth had been the instrument of freeing from a fate worse than death. Of this total, but eighteen were English; the remainder were almost wholly from the Mediterranean countries. On the 3d of September, just one week after the attack, the fleet sailed for England.

Profuse acknowledgment necessarily awaited the hero of a deed in which national exultation so happily blended with the sentiment of pity for the oppressed. The admiral was raised to the next rank in the peerage, and honors poured in upon him from every side—from abroad as well as from his own countrymen. His personal sense of the privilege permitted him, thus to crown a life of strenuous exertion by a martial deed of far-reaching beneficence, was a reward passing all others. In the opening words of his official report he voices his thankfulness: "In all the vicissitudes of a long life of public service, no circumstance has ever produced on my mind such impressions of gratitude and joy as the event of yesterday. To have been one of the humble instruments in the hands of Divine Providence for bringing to reason a ferocious Government, and destroying for ever the horrid system of Christian slavery, can never cease to be a source of delight and heartfelt comfort to every individual happy enough to be employed in it."

Here Lord Exmouth's career closes. Just forty years had elapsed since as a youth he had fought the *Carleton* on Lake Champlain, and he was yet to live sixteen in honored retreat; bearing, however, the burden of those whose occupation is withdrawn at an age too advanced to form new interests. Though in vigorous health and with ample fortune, "he would sometimes confess," says his biographer, "that he was happier amid his early difficulties." The idea of retirement, indeed, does not readily associate itself with the impression of prodigious vitality, which from first to last is produced by the record of his varied activities. In this respect, as in others, the contrast is marked between him and Saumarez, the two who more particularly illustrate the complementary sides of the brilliant group of naval leaders, in the second rank of distinction, which clustered around the great names of Nelson, Howe, and Jervis. In the old age of Saumarez, the even, ordered tenor of his active military life is reflected in the peaceful, satisfied enjoyment of repose and home happiness, of the fruits of labors past, which Collingwood, probably without good reason, fancied to be characteristic of his own temperament. Lord Exmouth, compelled to be a passive spectator, saw with consequent increased apprehension the internal political troubles of Great Britain in his later days. Though not a party man, he was strongly conservative, so that the agitations of the Reform era concealed from him the advantages towards which it was tending, and filled him with forebodings for the future of his country.

Like his distinguished contemporary, Admiral Saumarez, and like many others of those lion-hearted, masculine men who had passed their lives amid the storms of the elements and of battle—and like our own Farragut—Lord Exmouth was a deeply religious man. Strong as was his self-reliance in war and tempest, he rested upon the Almighty with the dependence of a child upon its father. His noble brother, Sir Israel Pellew, who had followed Nelson into the fire at Trafalgar, departed with the words, "I know in Whom I have believed;" and of the admiral himself, an officer who was often with him during the closing scene said, "I have seen him great in battle, but never so great as on his deathbed."

Lord Exmouth died on January 23, 1833. He was at the time Vice-Admiral of England, that distinguished honorary rank having been conferred upon him but a few months before his death.

NOTES

―――――――

Introduction

1. R. B. Watts, "The End of Sea Power," *USNI Proceedings*, Vol. 135, No. 9 (September 2009).
2. Geoffrey Till, *Seapower: A Guide for the Twenty-First Century* (New York: Routledge, 2009), 266.
3. Alfred Thayer Mahan, "Considerations Governing the Dispositions of Navies," in *Retrospect and Prospect: Studies in International Relations, Naval and Political* (Boston, MA: Little, Brown, and Company, 1908), 70.
4. Alfred Thayer Mahan, "A Twentieth Century Outlook," in *The Interest of America in Sea Power, Present and Future,* (Boston, MA: Little, Brown, and Company, 1897), 118.
5. Mahan, "Considerations Governing the Disposition of Navies," 71.
6. Alfred Thayer Mahan, "Preparedness for Naval War," in *The Interest of America in Sea Power, Present and Future* (Boston, MA: Little, Brown, and Company, 1897), 94.
7. Mahan, "Considerations Governing the Disposition of Navies," 68.
8. Mahan, "A Twentieth Century Outlook," 130.
9. Ibid., 126.
10. Mahan, "Considerations Governing the Dispositions of Navies," 71.
11. Mahan, "A Twentieth Century Outlook," 122.
12. Mahan, "Considerations Governing the Dispositions of Navies," 72.
13. Mahan, "A Twentieth Century Outlook," 122.
14. Ibid., 130.
15. Mahan, "Preparedness for Naval War," 114.
16. Mahan, "Considerations Governing the Dispositions of Navies," 72.
17. Alfred Thayer Mahan, "The Future in Relation to American Naval Power," in *The Interest of America in Sea Power, Present and Future* (Boston, MA: Little, Brown, and Company, 1897), 87.
18. Mahan, "Preparedness for Naval War," 96.
19. Ibid., 115.

20. Alfred Thayer Mahan, *Armaments and Arbitration, or The Place of Force in the International Relations of States* (New York, NY. Harper and Brothers, 1912), 206.

Chapter 1. Management, Administration, and Naval Leadership

1. Arthur K. Cebrowski and John J. Garstka, "Network-Centric Warfare: Its Origins and Future," *USNI Proceedings*, Vol. 124, No. 1 (January 1998).
2. Alfred Thayer Mahan, "Naval Education," *The Record of the U.S. Naval Institute*, Vol. 5, No. 4 (April 1879): 11.
3. Ibid., 13.
4. Ibid., 17.

Chapter 2. Globalization and the Fleet

1. Charles Carlisle Taylor, *The Life of Admiral Mahan, Naval Philosopher* (New York: George H. Dorn Company, 1920), 144.
2. Alfred Thayer Mahan, "Considerations Governing the Dispositions of Navies," in *Retrospect and Prospect: Studies in International Relations, Naval and Political* (Boston, MA: Little, Brown, and Company, 1908), 70.
3. Ibid., 71.
4. Ibid., 82.
5. Ibid., 97.

Chapter 3. Training of Officers and Sailors

1. Alfred Thayer Mahan, "The Principles of Naval Administration," in *Naval Administration and Warfare: Some General Principles* (Boston, MA: Little, Brown, and Company, 1918), 349.
2. Ibid., 352.
3. Ibid., 347.
4. Ibid., 327.
5. Ibid., 374.

Chapter 4. Leadership and Command

1. Alfred Thayer Mahan, "The Strength of Nelson," in *Naval Administration and Warfare: Some General Principles* (Boston, MA: Little, Brown, and Company, 1918), 161.
2. Ibid., 161.
3. Ibid., 159.

4. Ibid., 160.
5. Ibid., 163.
6. P. W. Singer, "Essay: The Rise of the Tactical General," *Armed Forces Journal,* June 2009.
7. This paper was read on the hundredth anniversary of the Battle of Trafalgar, October 21, 1905, before the Victorian Club, of Boston, U.S.A.

Chapter 5. History and Conventional Wisdom

1. Jon Sumida, "New Insights from Old Books," *Naval War College Review,* Vol. 54, No. 3 (2001), 110.

ABOUT THE EDITOR

LCDR Benjamin "BJ" Armstrong is a serving rotary-wing Naval Aviator in the U.S. Navy. He has served as a helicopter Detachment Officer-in-Charge, search and rescue, special warfare, and advanced instructor pilot. He holds a graduate degree in Military History from Norwich University and is a research student with Kings College, London. His articles on naval history and policy have appeared in a number of journals including *The Naval War College Review*, *Defense & Security Analysis*, and The U.S. Naval Institute's *Proceedings*.